Mike McGrath

PHP &
MySQL

in
easy steps

In easy steps is an imprint of In Easy Steps Limited
16 Hamilton Terrace· 42 Holly Walk · Leamington Spa
Warwickshire · United Kingdom · CV32 4LY
www.ineasysteps.com

Notice of Liability
Every effort has been made to ensure that this book contains accurate
and current information. However, In Easy Steps Limited and the
author shall not be liable for any loss or damage suffered by readers
as a result of any information contained herein.

Trademarks
All trademarks are acknowledged as belonging to their respective
companies.

In Easy Steps Limited supports The Forest Stewardship Council (FSC),
the leading international forest certification organisation. All our titles
that are printed on Greenpeace approved FSC certified paper carry the
FSC logo.

MIX
Paper from
responsible sources
FSC
www.fsc.org FSC® C020837

Printed and bound in the United Kingdom

ISBN 978-1-84078-537-1

Contents

Preface

The creation of this book has provided me, Mike McGrath, a welcome opportunity to demonstrate the latest server-side scripting techniques with PHP and MySQL databases. All examples I have given in this book demonstrate modern features of the PHP scripting language using the current MySQL Relational Database Management System that is supported on both Windows and Linux operating systems. I sincerely hope you enjoy discovering the exciting possibilities of PHP and MySQL and have as much fun with it as I did in writing this book.

In order to clarify the code listed in the steps given in each example I have adopted certain colorization conventions. Components of the PHP language are colored blue, programmer-specified names are red, numeric and string data values are black, and comments are green:

```php
<?php
        # Write the traditional greeting.
        $string = '<p>Hello World!</p>' ;
        echo $string ;
?>
```

Similarly, components of the SQL query language are colored blue, programmer-specified names are red, numeric and string data values are black, and comments are green:

```sql
# Insert 5 records into the "top_5_films" table.
INSERT INTO top_5_films ( position , title , year ) VALUES ( 1 , "Citizen Kane" , 1941 ) ;
```

Additionally, in order to identify each source code file described in the steps, a colored icon and file name appears in the margin alongside the steps:

script.php query.sql index.html style.css

For convenience I have placed source code files from the examples featured in this book into a single ZIP archive. You can obtain the complete archive by following these easy steps:

1 Browse to **http://www.ineasysteps.com** then navigate to the "Free Resources" and choose the "Downloads" section

2 Find "PHP & MySQL in easy steps" in the "Source Code" list, then click on the hyperlink entitled "All Code Examples" to download the archive

3 Now extract the archive contents to any convenient location on your computer

1

Getting started

Welcome to the exciting world of the data-driven web with PHP & MySQL. This chapter demonstrates how to create a dynamic development environment incorporating the Abyss Web Server, PHP engine, and MySQL database server.

Introducing PHP & MySQL

The most appealing modern websites provide a customized user experience by dynamically responding to some current conditions – user name, time of day, latest blog, shopping cart contents, etc. Many of these dynamic websites are created with PHP and MySQL.

What is PHP?

PHP is a widely-used general purpose scripting language that is especially suited for web development and can be embedded into HTML. It was created by programmer Rasmus Lerdorf as a set of scripts to maintain his website that he released as "Personal Home Page Tools (PHP Tools) version 1.0" on June 8, 1995. These were extended in the version 2 release of 1997, and the name changed to become a recursive acronym "PHP: Hypertext Preprocessor" in version 3 the following year. Performance, reliability, and extensibility was improved in 2000 with the release of PHP4, which was powered by the new Zend engine – a virtual machine. The current version PHP5 is powered by the Zend II engine and produced as free software by the PHP group. Today, PHP is installed on over 20 million websites and 1 million web servers.

What is MySQL?

MySQL is the world's most popular database software. It is used to manage stored data and is described as DataBase Management Software (DBMS) or Relational DataBase Management Software (RDBMS). MySQL was created by Michael Wildenius and David Axmark back in 1995. Its name ("My-S-Q-L" officially, but often pronounced "My Sequel") is a combination of Michael's daughter's name "My" and the term "SQL" (Structured Query Language). MySQL was originally produced by the company MySQL AB, founded by its creators, which was acquired by Sun Microsystems in 2008, and subsequently by Oracle in 2010. The current version MySQL 5.6 is powered by the InnoDB storage engine and the MySQL Community Server edition is available as free software. Today MySQL is used on some of the most frequently visited websites including Google, Wikipedia, Facebook and Twitter.

It is important to recognize that PHP and MySQL are both "server-side" technologies – that is to say they reside on the web server. They are not "client-side" technologies resident on the user's computer. So their magic takes place on "the cloud".

Understanding the cloud

Whenever a user asks to view a web page in their browser it requests the page from the web server, and receives the page in response, via the HTTP protocol. Where a web page contains PHP script the web server may first call upon the PHP engine to process the code and, if required, request data from a MySQL database before sending the response to the browser.

Hot tip

HTTP (HyperText Transfer Protocol) is the common communication standard that allows any computer connected to any web server to access files across the Web.

Don't forget

The examples in this book are created and tested with the listed software versions but may require modification for other versions.

The ensuing pages describe how to create a development environment for data-driven websites by installing the following server-side technologies on your own computer:

- Web Server – Abyss Web Server X1 Free Personal Edition
- PHP Engine – PHP 5.5.9
- MySQL Server – MySQL Community Server 5.6

9

Installing Abyss Web Server

Abyss X1 is a free compact web server available for Windows, Mac OS X, and Linux operating systems available for download at **aprelium.com**. Despite its small footprint, Abyss supports many powerful features including dynamic content generation with server-side scripts – so is an ideal companion for PHP & MySQL.

The Abyss Web Server can be installed on your own computer to provide an environment for PHP & MySQL website development.

1 Download the Abyss X1 Web Server setup package for your system from **aprelium.com/abyssws/downloads.php**

Further guidance on installation of the Abyss Web Server is available at **aprelium.com/abyssws/start.html**

Download the Personal Edition (Free - No expiration)

The latest version is **Abyss Web Server X1 (version 2.9.0.1)**

Download Abyss Web Server X1 for Windows (2112 KB)
(The setup package contains both 32-bit and 64-bit editions.)

Download Abyss Web Server X1 for Mac OS X (2014 KB)
(Universal Binary)

Download Abyss Web Server X1 for Linux (1991 KB)
(The setup package contains both 32-bit and 64-bit editions.)

2 Run the setup installer and accept the License terms, then choose to install with all suggested options

Don't forget

The Abyss setup package for Windows is an executable file named **abwsx1.exe** that you run to install the web server.

Abyss Web Server X1 Setup: Installation Op... ─ ☐ ✕

This will install Abyss Web Server X1 on your computer.

Select components to install:
- ☑ Abyss Web Server (64-bit)
- ☑ SSL Support
- ☑ ASP.NET Support
- ☑ Documentation
- ☑ Start Menu Shortcuts

Space required: 5.4MB

Cancel Version 2.9.0.1 < Back Next >

3 Accept the suggested location of **C:\Abyss Web Server** then choose to install Abyss as a Windows Service

Beware

If you choose the Manual Startup option the Abyss logo will not appear in your system tray for easy start/stop control and access to the server console. Instead, the console can be found with your browser at **http://localhost:9999**

4 Next, select your preferred language then enter a name and password for future access to the Abyss server console

5 Now, log in using your chosen name and password to see the Abyss console confirm the server status as Running

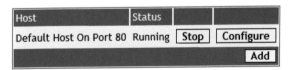

6 Finally, enter **http://localhost** into your browser address field then hit Return to see the default Abyss Welcome page get served up by the Abyss Web Server

Hot tip

In the Abyss console click the Configure button then the General icon to see the default HTTP Port is 80 and the default Documents Path (where your web pages will reside) is **/htdocs**.

Installing the PHP engine

The PHP interpreter "engine", which implements PHP scripts within web pages, is available for Windows, Mac OS X, and Linux operating systems as a free download at **php.net**

Additionally, a pre-configured package for the Abyss Web Server on Windows is available from **aprelium.com** and is recommended for a simple fast installation.

Further guidance on installation of PHP is available at **php.net/manual/en/install.php**

1 Download the PHP setup package for your system from **aprelium.com/downloads**

2 Run the downloaded executable file to launch the Setup Wizard then click on the Next button to begin

3 Next, accept the License terms then click on the Next button to proceed with the installation

4 Now, accept the suggested location of **C:\Program Files\ PHP5** then click the Install button to continue

Hot tip

The PHP installation location will be required when configuring the Abyss Web Server for PHP – make a note of the Destination Folder.

5 Finally, after the installation completes, click on the Finish button to close the Setup Wizard

Don't forget

Following installation of PHP the web server cannot yet execute PHP scripts until it is configured to recognize them and to find the PHP interpreter engine – all as described on the next page.

13

Configuring Abyss for PHP

The Abyss Web Server must be configured to recognize PHP scripts and employ the PHP interpreter when it encounters them. This is achieved in the Abyss server console by associating the file extension ".php" as being PHP scripts and by specifying the location of the PHP engine on your system to interpret them.

Further guidance on configuration of the Abyss Web Server is available online at **aprelium.com/abyssws/ start.html**

14

1 Enter **http://localhost:9999** into your browser address field (or click on the Abyss logo in your system tray) to launch the Abyss server console, then click the Configure button to open its Configuration page

Host	Status		
Default Host On Port 80	Running	Stop	Configure
			Add

2 Next, click on the 🗒 Scripting Parameters icon to open the Scripting Parameters page for editing

3 Ensure that the Enable Scripts Execution box is checked, then click the Add button in the Interpreters table to open the Interpreters-Add page

4 Now, set the Interface to "FastCGI", the Interpreter to the location of the PHP interpreter (**php-cgi.exe**) on your system, and Add the file Extension "php" then click OK

Interface ⓘ:	FastCGI (Local - Pipes) ▾
Interpreter ⓘ:	C:\Program Files (x86)\PHP5\php-cgi.exe Browse...
Arguments ⓘ:	
Advanced Parameters ⓘ:	Edit...
	☑ Check for file existence before execution ⓘ
Type ⓘ:	Standard ▾
	☑ Use the associated extensions to automatically update the Script Paths ⓘ
Associated Extensions ⓘ:	Extension
	php ✎ 🗑
	Add

5 Click the Restart button in the Console window to apply the changes you have made to the Abyss configuration

The configuration has changed. Press Restart to apply the modifications.

The Abyss Web Server should now be running on your system correctly configured to recognize that documents having the **.php** file extension should be interpreted by the PHP engine. Configuration can now be tested by creating a simple PHP script for service to your web browser by Abyss.

6 Open a plain text editor and exactly type the script below
`<?php phpinfo() ?>`

7 Save the script as **phpinfo.php** in the Abyss document path directory, typically at **C:\Abyss Web Server\htdocs**

8 Exactly enter the location **http://localhost/phpinfo.php** into your web browser's address field to see Abyss serve up a web page containing your PHP version information

Don't forget

PHP scripts are case-sensitive so you must copy the listed script using lowercase characters only.

phpinfo.php

Beware

Documents can only be interpreted by the PHP engine if served up by the web server using the HTTP protocol. You cannot simply open a PHP file in your browser directly. Always use the location **http://localhost/**

Embedding PHP script

PHP script may be embedded within HTML documents – meaning PHP and HTML code can both happily co-exist in the same file. All embedded PHP code must be contained within **<?php** and **?>** tags so it can be readily recognized by the PHP engine for interpretation. Typically, the PHP code will write content into the body section of the HTML document, which is then sent to the web browser.

hello.php

1 Launch a plain text editor and create this valid barebones HTML5 document with an empty body section
```
<!DOCTYPE HTML>
<html lang="en">
<head><meta charset="UTF-8">
<title>Getting Started With PHP</title>
</head>
<body>

</body>
</html>
```

2 Insert tags into the body section to contain PHP code
```
<?php

?>
```

3 Now, insert between the PHP tags a descriptive comment and a line of code to write content into the body section
```
# Write the traditional greeting.
echo '<h1>Hello World!</h1>' ;
```

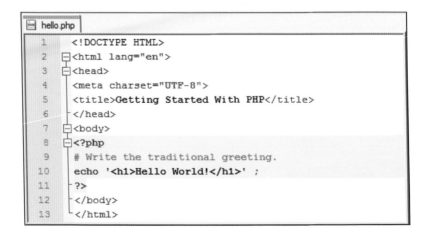

```
hello.php
1    <!DOCTYPE HTML>
2    <html lang="en">
3    <head>
4      <meta charset="UTF-8">
5      <title>Getting Started With PHP</title>
6    </head>
7    <body>
8    <?php
9      # Write the traditional greeting.
10     echo '<h1>Hello World!</h1>' ;
11   ?>
12   </body>
13   </html>
```

16

4 Set the document encoding to UTF-8 format then save it as **hello.php** in the Abyss server's **/htdocs** folder

5 Next, enter the location **http://localhost/hello.php** into your web browser's address field to see Abyss serve up a web page containing content written by embedded PHP code

6 Now, use your web browser's View Source facility to see that PHP has written the content into the body section, including the HTML **<h1></h1>** heading tags

PHP script can be embedded in earlier versions of HTML in just the same way. Other examples in this book demonstrate embedded PHP script but do not repeatedly list the HTML code.

Beware

Windows' Notepad automatically adds a hidden "Byte Order Mark" (BOM) to the file, while other editors (such as Notepad++ shown here) allow this to be omitted. Notepad++ can be freely downloaded from **notepad-plus-plus.org**

Don't forget

The PHP **echo** instruction statement literally writes the entire content contained within the pair of ' single quote marks. Like all other PHP statements it must be terminated by a ; semi-colon character.

17

Installing the MySQL Server

The MySQL database server, which provides "back-end" storage for data-driven websites, is available for Windows, Mac OS X, and Linux operating systems as a free download at **mysql.com**

Further guidance on installation of the MySQL Server is available at **http://dev.mysql.com/ doc/refman/5.6/en/ installing.html**

1 Download the MySQL Community Edition installer for your system from **mysql.com/downloads/mysql**

2 Run the installer and select "Developer Default" when asked to choose a Setup Type

3 Ensure you have an internet connection then allow the installer to download any missing setup requirements

MySQL Installer

The MySQL Installer can be launched at any time from the Start Menu to change the configuration or to install updates.

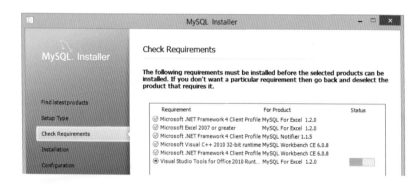

4 When all requirements have been downloaded push the Execute button to install MySQL on your system

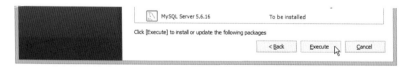

After installation the MySQL Server must then be configured.

5 Next, choose "Development Machine" as the Server Type to begin the MySQL Configuration process

Beware

By default, the MySQL Server uses port 3306. If you are running a firewall you may need to specifically allow the MySQL Server connections via this port. Refer to your firewall documentation for further guidance.

6 Then, enter a root user password of your choice twice into the Password fields and click Next

7 Now, accept the suggested Windows Service Name and choose to run the service as a Standard System Account to complete configuration of the MySQL installation

Hot tip

Ensure that your MySQL Server Configuration completes successfully before continuing. If necessary repeat the installation process.

Employing the MySQL Client

After installation of the MySQL Server as a Windows service, described on the previous page, you can communicate with databases via the MySQL Command Line Client that gets installed with the server package. Upon its launch it will first request the root user password you chose during installation. Once the password has been verified, the MySQL Command Line Client then presents a **mysql>** command prompt from which you can create and manipulate databases.

 Launch the MySQL Command Line Client from the MySQL group that has been added to the Start menu, then enter the root password you chose during installation

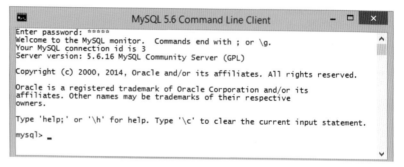

```
Enter password: *****
Welcome to the MySQL monitor.  Commands end with ; or \g.
Your MySQL connection id is 3
Server version: 5.6.16 MySQL Community Server (GPL)

Copyright (c) 2000, 2014, Oracle and/or its affiliates. All rights reserved.

Oracle is a registered trademark of Oracle Corporation and/or its
affiliates. Other names may be trademarks of their respective
owners.

Type 'help;' or '\h' for help. Type '\c' to clear the current input statement.

mysql> _
```

 At the **mysql>** command prompt, precisely issue this command to create a new database named "site_db"
CREATE DATABASE IF NOT EXISTS site_db ;

3 Now, precisely issue a further command to display all databases that now exist on your MySQL Server
SHOW DATABASES ;

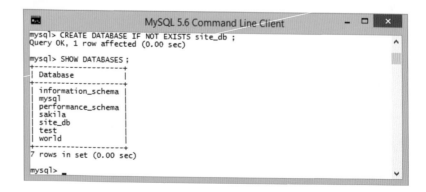

```
mysql> CREATE DATABASE IF NOT EXISTS site_db ;
Query OK, 1 row affected (0.00 sec)

mysql> SHOW DATABASES ;
+--------------------+
| Database           |
+--------------------+
| information_schema |
| mysql              |
| performance_schema |
| sakila             |
| site_db            |
| test               |
| world              |
+--------------------+
7 rows in set (0.00 sec)

mysql> _
```

Creating MySQL users

While the MySQL root user is allowed complete control over the databases on the MySQL Server, it is obviously inadvisable to allow other users such freedom for best security of the databases. The root user can therefore create users with specific "privileges" controlling what actions they may perform on the MySQL Server. For example, you may typically wish to allow database users the ability to retrieve, add, and amend data but deny them the ability to modify the database's structure or remove it from the server.

The root user can create a user in the MySQL Command Line Client by issuing a "grant" statement that identifies the user and specifies the privileges they are allowed for particular databases. The grant statement has this syntax:

GRANT *privileges* **ON** *database-name*.*
TO '*user-name*'**@**'*host-name*' **IDENTIFIED BY** '*password*' ;

The privileges are specified as a comma-separated list of keywords which that user may use when accessing the specified database. For instance, basic privileges to **SELECT**, **INSERT**, and **UPDATE**.

Beware

MySQL is case-sensitive and requires precise syntax – you must be sure to use correct spacing and letter case as it appears listed. For example, do not leave spaces around the @ character that defines the user name and host.

1 Log into the MySQL Command Line Client as the root user then precisely issue this command to create a user with basic privileges to access the whole "site_db" database
GRANT SELECT, INSERT, UPDATE ON site_db.*
TO 'mike'@'localhost' IDENTIFIED BY 'easysteps' ;

Hot tip

Note that the password gets stored in encrypted format for security.

2 Now, issue a command to confirm the new user has been added and to reveal that user's access privileges
SHOW GRANTS FOR 'mike'@'localhost' ;

```
                          MySQL 5.6 Command Line Client                    _  □  ×

mysql> GRANT SELECT, INSERT, UPDATE ON site_db.* TO 'mike'@'localhost' IDENTIFIED BY 'easysteps';
Query OK, 0 rows affected (0.00 sec)

mysql> SHOW GRANTS FOR 'mike'@'localhost';
+-----------------------------------------------------------------------------------------------+
| Grants for mike@localhost                                                                     |
+-----------------------------------------------------------------------------------------------+
| GRANT USAGE ON *.* TO 'mike'@'localhost' IDENTIFIED BY PASSWORD '*0864A0E51F8418711EEB808FA55210A3F2917007' |
| GRANT SELECT, INSERT, UPDATE ON `site_db`.* TO 'mike'@'localhost'                             |
+-----------------------------------------------------------------------------------------------+
2 rows in set (0.00 sec)

mysql> _
```

Connecting MySQL with PHP

Connection to a MySQL database can be attempted in PHP with a standard piece of script that describes four connection parameters of host, user name, password, and database name. Upon failure the script provides a descriptive message, whereas on success it specifies the character set to to be used when sending data to and from the database server:

```
$dbc = mysqli_connect ( 'host', 'user', 'password', 'database' )
  OR die ( mysqli_connect_error() ) ;
mysqli_set_charset( $dbc, 'charset' ) ;
```

You need not understand in detail how the script works at this stage but recognize that it contains sensitive information. For this reason it should not be placed in the web server's /htdocs directory like all other PHP scripts, where its contents may be accessible, but placed instead safely in /htdocs parent directory. For example, in the "C:/Abyss Web Server" directory rather than in the "C:/Abyss Web Server/htdocs" directory.

Any PHP script can incorporate another PHP script by using a "require" statement to specify the other script's path. This feature can be used to good effect to incorporate the connection script without revealing its sensitive information.

connect_db.php

1. Launch a plain text editor and create a connection script describing the parameters from the previous pages
```
<?php
```

```
# Connect  on 'localhost' for user 'mike'
# with password 'easysteps' to database 'site_db'.
$dbc = mysqli_connect
  ( 'localhost' , 'mike' , 'easysteps' , 'site_db' )
OR die
  ( mysqli_connect_error() ) ;
```

```
# Set encoding to match PHP script encoding.
mysqli_set_charset( $dbc , 'utf8' ) ;
```

2. Save the file in the parent directory of your web server's /htdocs directory folder as connect_db.php

③ Now, begin a second script that incorporates the connection script, stating its path in the parent directory

```php
<?php
# Incorporate the MySQL connection script.
require ( '../connect_db.php' ) ;
```

require.php

④ Next, complete this script by adding instructions to display connection information if the attempt has succeeded

```php
# Display MySQL version and host.
if( mysqli_ping( $dbc ) )
{ echo 'MySQL Server ' . mysqli_get_server_info( $dbc ).
            ' on ' . mysqli_get_host_info( $dbc ) ; }
```

⑤ Save the script in your web server's **/htdocs** directory as **require.php** then open it in your browser (via HTTP) to see the connection details on successful connection

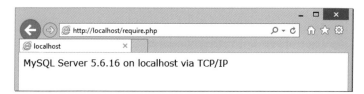

⑥ Temporarily edit **connect_db.php** by changing the database name to one that does not exist then save the file and reload the page in your browser to see the error

Don't forget

You do not need to understand how these scripts work just now – they merely ensure you can connect to MySQL with PHP. But you can usefully refer back to them later to see how your knowledge of PHP has progressed.

⑦ Finally, correct the **connect_db.php** script by changing the database name back to **site_db** then save the file and reload the page to see the connection succeed once more

Congratulations, you have now successfully configured the Abyss Web Server, PHP engine, and MySQL Server for development.

23

Summary

- PHP is a scripting language that is especially suited for web development as it can be embedded in HTML

- MySQL is Relational DataBase Management Software (RDBMS) that can provide back-end data storage for websites

- PHP and MySQL are both server-side technologies that deliver data-driven websites to the browser from the cloud

- A local development environment can be created by installing a Web Server, the PHP engine, and the MySQL Server

- The Web Server must be configured to recognize scripts so it will direct them to the PHP engine for interpretation

- All embedded PHP code must be contained within **<?php** and **?>** tags so it can be readily recognized by the PHP engine

- Documents containing PHP script can best be encoded using the popular UTF-8 character format

- The MySQL Server can be installed on Windows systems as a background service so it is always readily available

- The MySQL Command Line Client gets installed with the Server package and can create and manipulate databases

- The root user password chosen during installation of MySQL can be used to launch the MySQL Command Line Client

- MySQL users can be created by root with privileges specifying what actions they may perform on the MySQL Server

- A grant statement identifies the user by name and password and specifies their privileges allowed for particular databases

- Connection to a MySQL database can be attempted in PHP with a standard piece of script that describes connection parameters of host, user name, password, and database name

- Any PHP script can incorporate another PHP script by using a require statement stating the other script's path

2 Performing operations

This chapter demonstrates how to store and manipulate data using PHP operators.

Creating variables

A "variable" is a named container in a PHP script in which a data value can be stored. The stored value can be referenced using the variable's name and changed (varied) as the script proceeds. The script author can choose any name for a variable providing it adheres to these three naming conventions:

- Names must begin with a $ dollar sign – for example **$name**

- Names can comprise letters, numbers, and underscore characters, but not spaces – for example **$subtotal_1**

- The first character after the $ dollar sign must be a letter or an underscore character – it cannot be a number

Note that variable names in PHP are case-sensitive so **$name**, **$Name**, and **$NAME** are three separate individual variables.

PHP variables are "loosely typed" meaning they can contain data of any type, unlike "strongly typed" variables in some languages where the data type must be specified when the variable is created. So, a PHP variable may happily contain an integer number, or a floating-point number, or a string of text characters, or a Boolean value of **TRUE** or **FALSE**, or an object, or a **NULL** empty value.

A variable is created in a PHP script simply by stating its name. The variable can then be assigned an initial value (initialized) by using the = assignment operator to state its value. This statement, and all others in PHP, must end with a semi-colon like this:

$body_temp = 98.6 ;

The value contained within the variable can then be displayed by referencing it using the variable name like this:

echo $body_temp ;

Usefully, the variable's value can be displayed as part of a mixed string by enclosing the string and variable name in <u>double quotes</u>:

echo "Body temperature is $body_temp degrees Fahrenheit" ;

The double quotes ensure that PHP will evaluate the whole string and substitute named variables with their stored values. This feature does not work if the string is enclosed in single quotes!

Beware

Do not confuse the purpose of double and single quotes. Remember that PHP only makes variable substitutions for mixed strings enclosed within double quotes.

① Create a valid HTML document, like the one listed on page 16, then insert PHP tags into the body section
```
<?php
  # Statements to be inserted here.
?>
```

variable.php

② Now, insert between the PHP tags a statement to create and initialize a variable
```
$body_temp = 98.6 ;
```

③ Next, insert a statement to display the variable value alone
```
echo $body_temp ;
```

Hot tip

Notice that variables created in the main body of a script, like the one in this example, are accessible "globally" throughout the entire PHP script.

④ Then, insert a statement to display the variable value substituted in a mixed string – assigned in double quotes
```
echo "<p>Body temperature is $body_temp
                degrees Fahrenheit " ;
```

⑤ Insert a statement to assign a new value to the variable
```
$body_temp = 37.0 ;
```

27

⑥ Finally, insert a statement to display the new variable value substituted in a mixed string
```
echo "( $body_temp degrees Celsius )</p>" ;
```

⑦ Save the document in your web browser's **/htdocs** directory as **variable.php** then open the page via HTTP to see the variable values get displayed

Don't forget

Each statement in the PHP language must be terminated by a semi-colon – just as each statement in the English language must be terminated by a period.

```
98.6

Body temperature is 98.6 degrees Fahrenheit ( 37 degrees Celsius )
```

Managing strings

A "string" of text can be stored in a variable in much the same way as a numeric value but the assignment must surround the string with quote marks to denote its beginning and end. Both single and double quote marks can be used for this purpose but you must use the same type of quote marks to denote the beginning and end of the text string. For example, both these statements make valid string assignments:

$song_title = "Summertime Blues" ;

$song_title = 'Summertime Blues' ;

Where you wish to store a string of text that itself includes quote marks you can "escape" the included quote marks by preceding them with a \ backslash character, or use the alternative type of quote mark within the string. For example, both these statements assign strings that include quote marks:

$song_title = "the \"Summertime\" aria by George Gershwin" ;

$song_title = 'the "Summertime" aria by George Gershwin' ;

The second technique, using double quote marks within the string, is easier to read and is preferred throughout this book.

String values can be displayed as part of a mixed string by enclosing the mixed string in <u>double quotes</u> like this:

echo "Many regard $song_title as a popular classic" ;

Don't forget

Variable names cannot contain spaces – but the underscore character is often used in their place.

The double quotes ensure that PHP will evaluate the mixed string and substitute named variables with their stored values. This feature does not work if the string is enclosed in single quotes!

String values can be joined together ("concatenated") into a single string using the . period concatenation operator like this:

$hi = 'Hello' ;
$bye = 'Goodbye' ;
$song_title = $hi . $bye ; # 'HelloGoodbye'

Additionally, spaces and punctuation can usefully be inserted when concatenating strings, so the title assignment above could be modified to include a comma and a space:

$song_title = $hi . ', ' . $bye ; # 'Hello, Goodbye'

string.php

1 Create a valid HTML document, like the one listed on page 16, then insert PHP tags into the body section
```
<?php
    # Statements to be inserted here.
?>
```

2 Now, insert between the PHP tags a statement to create and initialize two variables
```
$phrase = 'The truth is rarely pure' ;
$author = 'Oscar Wilde' ;
```

3 Next, insert a statement to display a variable value alone
```
echo $phrase ;
```

4 Then, insert a statement to display the variable value substituted in a mixed string – assigned in double quotes
```
echo "<p>It is often said that <q>$phrase</q> </p>" ;
```

5 Insert a statement to concatenate a string to a variable
```
$phrase = $phrase . ' and never simple' ;
```

6 Finally, insert a statement to display both current variable values substituted in a mixed string
```
echo "<p><q>$phrase</q><cite>$author</cite></p>" ;
```

7 Save the document in your web browser's **/htdocs** directory as **string.php** then open the page via HTTP to see the variable values get displayed

Hot tip

You can also use a shorthand concatenate assignment operator **.=** to join two strings – so that **$a = $a . $b** can be simply written **$a .= $b**.

29

Hot tip

Adopt a consistent naming style for your variables – such as all lowercase **$my_var**, or "camelcase" **$myVar**.

Producing arrays

An array variable can store multiple items of data in sequential array "elements" that are numbered ("indexed") starting at zero. So, the first array value is stored in array element number zero. Individual array element values can be referenced using the variable name followed by the index number in square brackets. For example, **$months[0]** references the value stored in the first array element, **$months[1]** references the value stored in the second array element, and so on.

Variable arrays can be created by making multiple statements that assign values to successive elements, or by making a single statement using a PHP **array()** function to fill the elements:

```
$months[] = 'January' ;
$months[] = 'February' ;
$months[] = 'March' ;
```

```
$months = array( 'January' , 'February' , 'March' ) ;
```

Both create an array where the value stored in each element can be referenced using its index number, such as **$months[0]**.

When creating an array you can optionally specify a key name for each element that can be used to reference that element's value:

```
$months['jan'] = 'January' ;
$months['feb'] = 'February' ;
$months['mar'] = 'March' ;
```

```
$months =
array( 'jan' => 'January' , 'feb' => 'February' , 'mar' => 'March' ) ;
```

Both create an array where the value stored in each element can be referenced using its key name, such as **$months['jan']**.

All elements of an array can be accessed using a **foreach** loop to reference each element's value in turn and assign it to a variable:

```
foreach( $months as $value )
{
  # Use the current $value on each iteration.
}
```

The keys can also be accessed on each iteration of the loop using
```
foreach( $months as $key => $value )
{
  # Use the current $key and $value on each iteration.
}
```

① Create a valid HTML document, like the one listed on page 16, then insert PHP tags into the body section
```php
<?php
# Statements to be inserted here.
?>
```

array.php

② Now, insert between the PHP tags a statement to create and initialize a variable array with values
```php
$days = array( 'Monday' , 'Tuesday' , 'Wednesday' ) ;
```

③ Next, insert a statement to display the value in all array elements as a bulleted list
```php
foreach( $days as $value ) { echo "&bull; $value " ; }
```

④ Then, insert a statement to create and initialize a variable array with both keys and values
```php
$months = array( 'jan' => 'January' ,
                 'feb' => 'February' , 'mar' => 'March' ) ;
```

⑤ Finally, insert statements to display the key and value in all elements as a definition list
```php
echo '<dl>' ;
foreach( $months as $key => $value )
{ echo "<dt>$key<dd>$value" ; }
echo '</dl>' ;
```

⑥ Save the document in your web browser's **/htdocs** directory as **array.php** then open the page via HTTP to see the variable array element values get displayed

31

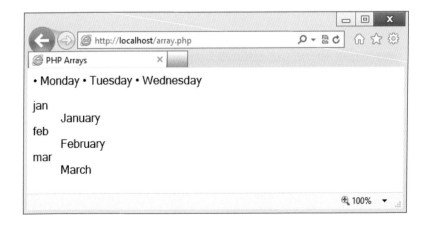

```
http://localhost/array.php
PHP Arrays

• Monday • Tuesday • Wednesday
jan
      January
feb
      February
mar
      March

                                          100%
```

Sorting arrays

PHP provides two handy functions to convert between variable arrays and strings because they are so frequently used together. The **implode()** function converts an array to a string and inserts a specified separator between each value. Typically, this might be used to create a list of comma-separated values like this:

$csv_list = implode(' , ' , $array) ;

Conversely, the **explode()** function converts a string to an array by specifying a separator around which to break up the string. This might be used to create an array from a comma-separated list:

$array = explode(' , ' . $csv_list) ;

PHP also provides three useful functions to sort array elements into ascending alphanumeric order (a-z 1-9):

- **sort()** function – sorts by value discarding the original key

- **asort()** function – sorts by value retaining the original key

- **ksort()** function – sorts by key

Existing array values are sorted with a simple statement like this:

$makers = array('Ford' , 'Chevrolet' , 'Dodge') ;
sort($makers) ;

Array elements can also be sorted into descending alphanumeric order (9-1 z-a) with three similar functions:

- **rsort()** function – sorts by value discarding the original key

- **arsort()** function – sorts by value retaining the original key

- **krsort()** function – sorts by key

It is important to recognize that specified key names will be discarded by the **sort()** and **rsort()** functions so these should only be used where the key/value relationship is not significant – otherwise use the **asort()** and **arsort()** functions to retain the keys.

① Create a valid HTML document, like the one listed on page 16, then insert PHP tags into the body section
```php
<?php
    # Statements to be inserted here.
?>
```

sort.php

② Now, insert between the PHP tags a statement to create and initialize a variable array with key names and values
```php
$cars = array( 'Dodge' => 'Viper' ,
        'Chevrolet' => 'Camaro' , 'Ford' => 'Mustang' ) ;
```

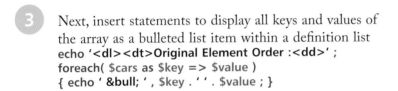

Hot tip

You can discover the number of elements in an array with a **count()** function. For example,
$num = count($array) ;

③ Next, insert statements to display all keys and values of the array as a bulleted list item within a definition list
```php
echo '<dl><dt>Original Element Order :<dd>' ;
foreach( $cars as $key => $value )
{ echo ' &bull; ' , $key . ' ' . $value ; }
```

④ Then, insert statements to display the array sorted by value
```php
asort( $cars ) ;
echo '<dt>Sorted Into Value Order :<dd>' ;
foreach( $cars as $key => $value )
{ echo ' &bull; ' , $key . ' ' . $value ; }
```

33

⑤ Finally, insert statements to display the array sorted by key
```php
ksort( $cars ) ;
echo '<dt>Sorted Into Key Order :<dd>' ;
foreach( $cars as $key => $value )
{ echo ' &bull; ' , $key . ' ' . $value ; }
echo '</dl>' ;
```

Don't forget

Do not use the **sort()** or **rsort()** functions where the keys are important.

⑥ Save the document in your web browser's **/htdocs** directory as **sort.php** then open the page via HTTP to see the sorted array values get displayed

Describing dimensions

The numbering of array elements is more correctly known as the "array index" and, because element numbering starts at zero, is sometimes referred to as a "zero-based index". An array created with a single index is a one-dimensional array in which the elements appear in a single row:

Element content...	A	B	C	D	E
Index numbers...	[0]	[1]	[2]	[3]	[4]

Arrays can also have multiple indices – to represent multiple dimensions. An array created with two indices is a two-dimensional array in which the elements appear in multiple rows:

First index	[0]	A	B	C	D	E
	[1]	F	G	H	I	J
Second index		[0]	[1]	[2]	[3]	[4]

With multi-dimensional arrays the value contained in each element is referenced by stating the number of each index. For example, with the two-dimensional array above, the element at [1][2] contains the letter H.

Two-dimensional arrays are useful to store grid-based information, such as XY coordinates. Creating a three-dimensional array, with three indices, would allow XYZ coordinates to be stored.

Creating a multi-dimensional array in PHP is simply a matter of creating an outer array whose elements are themselves arrays. As usual you may optionally specify a key name for each element – in this case to represent each inner array. Individual values can then be referenced using the key name and inner index number:

$matrix['Letter'][0]

It is, however, necessary to always enclose array variables that use quoted keys within curly braces when included in a string:

echo "Element value is {$matrix['Letter'][0]} " ;

All inner arrays in a multi-dimensional array can be accessed using a **foreach** loop to iterate through the arrays. A nested **foreach** loop can then reference each element in turn.

Beware

Multi-dimensional arrays with more than two indices can produce hard to read source code and may lead to errors.

① Create a valid HTML document, like the one listed on page 16, then insert PHP tags into the body section
```php
<?php
    # Statements to be inserted here.
?>
```

matrix.php

② Now, insert between the PHP tags a statement to create and initialize two regular variable arrays and a two-dimensional array with key names
```php
$letters = array( 'A' , 'B' , 'C' ) ;
$numbers = array( 1 , 2 , 3 ) ;
$matrix =
array( 'Letter' => $letters , 'Number' => $numbers ) ;
```

Hot tip

Multi-dimensional arrays are more common than you might think. For example, an HTML form that allows multiple selections for inputs with the same name are submitted as a multi-dimensional array.

③ Next, insert a statement to display a single stored value
```php
echo "<p>Start : {$matrix['Letter'][0]} </p>" ;
```

④ Finally, insert statements to display the key and value in all elements as two unordered lists
```php
foreach( $matrix as $array => $list )
{
  echo '<ul>' ;
  foreach( $list as $key => $value )
  { echo "<li>$array [ $key ] = $value" ; }
  echo '</ul>' ;
}
```

35

⑤ Save the document in your web browser's **/htdocs** directory as **matrix.php** then open the page via HTTP to see the variable array values get displayed

Don't forget

Array variables that use quoted keys must be enclosed within curly braces when included in a string.

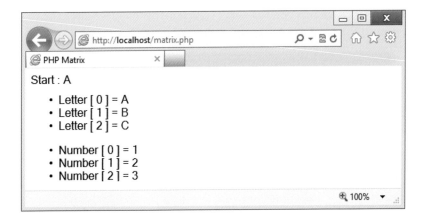

```
http://localhost/matrix.php
PHP Matrix

Start : A

  • Letter [ 0 ] = A
  • Letter [ 1 ] = B
  • Letter [ 2 ] = C

  • Number [ 0 ] = 1
  • Number [ 1 ] = 2
  • Number [ 2 ] = 3

                                        100%
```

Doing arithmetic

The arithmetic operators commonly used in PHP scripts are listed in the table below, together with the operation they perform:

Operator:	Operation:
+	Addition
-	Subtraction
*	Multiplication
/	Division
%	Modulus
++	Increment
--	Decrement

Operators for addition, subtraction, multiplication, and division act as you would expect. Care must be taken, however, to group expressions for clarity where more than one operator is used:

a = b * c - d % e / f ; # This is unclear.

a = (b * c) - ((d % e) / f) ; # This is clearer.

The % modulus operator divides the first given number by the second given number and returns the remainder of the operation. This is useful to determine if a number has an odd or even value. The ++ increment operator and -- decrement operator alter the given number by one and return the resulting new value. These are most often used to count iterations in a loop. The increment operator increases the value by one and the decrement operator decreases the value by one.

Shorthand expressions can usefully be created by combining an arithmetic operator with the = assignment operator. For example:

```
a += b ;        # Equivalent to a = ( a + b ) ;
a -= b ;        # Equivalent to a = ( a - b ) ;
a *= b ;        # Equivalent to a = ( a * b ) ;
a /= b ;        # Equivalent to a = ( a / b ) ;
```

1 Create a valid HTML document, like the one listed on page 16, then insert PHP tags into the body section

```php
<?php
   # Statements to be inserted here.
?>
```

arithmetic.php

2 Now, insert between the PHP tags statements to create and initialize two variables

```php
$a = 4 ;
$b = 8 ;
```

3 Next, insert statements to display the results of arithmetical operations using the variable values

```php
$result = $a + $b ; echo "Addition : $result <br>" ;
$result = $b - $a ; echo "Subtraction : $result <br>" ;
$result = $a * $b ; echo "Multiplication : $result <br>" ;
$result = $b / $a ; echo "Division : $result <br>" ;
$result = $a % $b ; echo "Modulo : $result <br>" ;
```

4 Finally, insert statements to increment and decrement the values stored in the variables

```php
$a++ ; echo "Increment : $a <br>" ;
$b-- ; echo "Decrement : $b <br>" ;
```

5 Save the document in your web browser's **/htdocs** directory as **arithmetic.php** then open the page via HTTP to see the results and variable values get displayed

Hot tip

PHP has some useful functions to work with numbers. For example, **round($n)** rounds **$n** to the nearest integer and **number_format($n)** adds commas to **$n** denoting groups of thousands.

37

Beware

Notice that the variable value is immediately increased only with the prefix increment operator – with the postfix operator it is incremented the next time it is referenced.

Comparing values

The operators that are commonly used in PHP scripts to compare two values are listed in the table below:

Operator:	Comparative test:
==	Equality
!=	Inequality
>	Greater than
<	Less than
>=	Greater than or equal to
<=	Less than or equal to
?:	TRUE or FALSE

The == equality operator compares two operands and returns a Boolean **TRUE** result if both are numerically equal in value, otherwise it returns **FALSE**. Characters and strings are also compared numerically by their ASCII code value. Conversely, the != inequality operator returns **TRUE** if the two operands are <u>not</u> equal, otherwise it returns **FALSE**.

The > "greater than" operator compares two operands and returns **TRUE** if the first is greater in value than the second, or it returns **FALSE** if it is equal or less in value. The < "less than" operator makes the same comparison but returns **TRUE** if the first operand is less in value than the second, otherwise it returns **FALSE**. Adding the = operator after a > "greater than" or < "less than" operator makes it also return **TRUE** when the two operands are exactly equal.

The ?: ternary operator evaluates an expression for a **TRUE** or **FALSE** Boolean value then executes one of two statements depending on the result of the evaluation. An appropriate returned value can be assigned to a variable using this syntax:

```
$var = ( expression ) ? if-TRUE-return-this : if-FALSE-return this ;
```

Hot tip

Equality and inequality operators are useful in testing the state of two variables to perform conditional branching in a PHP script.

① Create a valid HTML document, like the one listed on page 16, then insert PHP tags into the body section

```php
<?php
    # Statements to be inserted here.
?>
```

comparison.php

② Now, insert between the PHP tags statements to create and initialize five variables

```php
$zero = 0 ; $nil = 0 ; $one = 1 ; $upr = 'A' ; $lwr = 'a' ;
```

③ Next, insert statements to display equality comparisons

```php
$result = ( $zero == $nil ) ? 'TRUE' : 'FALSE' ;
        echo "0==0 is $result <br>" ;
$result = ( $zero == $one ) ? 'TRUE' : 'FALSE'  ;
        echo "0==1 is : $result <br>" ;
$result = ( $upr == $lwr ) ? 'TRUE' : 'FALSE'  ;
        echo "A==a is $result <br>" ;
$result = ( $upr != $lwr ) ? 'TRUE' : 'FALSE'  ;
        echo "A!=a is $result <hr>" ;
```

④ Finally, insert statements to display greater comparisons

```php
$result = ( $one > $nil ) ? 'TRUE' : 'FALSE'  ;
        echo "1>0 is $result <br>" ;
$result = ( $zero >= $nil ) ? 'TRUE' : 'FALSE'  ;
        echo "0>=0 is $result <br>" ;
$result = ( $one <= $nil ) ? 'TRUE' : 'FALSE'  ;
        echo "1<=0 is $result <br>" ;
```

⑤ Save the document in your web browser's **/htdocs** directory as **comparison.php** then open the page via HTTP to see the results get displayed

Hot tip

A Boolean **TRUE** value is represented numerically by 1 in PHP language.

Hot tip

The ASCII code value for uppercase '**A**' is 65 and for lowercase '**a**' it's 97 – so their comparison here returns **FALSE**.

Assessing logic

The logical operators most commonly used in PHP scripts are listed in the table below:

Operator:	Operation:
&&	Logical AND
AND	Logical AND (alternative form of **&&**)
\|\|	Logical OR
OR	Logical OR (alternative form of **\|\|**)
!	Logical NOT

The logical operators are used with operands that have the Boolean values of **TRUE** or **FALSE**, or an expression that can convert to **TRUE** or **FALSE**.

The logical **&&** AND operator will evaluate two operands and return **TRUE** only if both operands are themselves **TRUE**. Otherwise the **&&** AND operator will return **FALSE**. This is used in conditional branching where the direction of a PHP script is determined by testing two conditions. If both conditions are satisfied the program will go in a certain direction, otherwise it will take a different direction.

Unlike the **&&** AND operator that needs both operands to be **TRUE** the **\|\|** OR operator will evaluate two operands and return **TRUE** if either one of the operands is itself **TRUE**. If neither operand is **TRUE** then the **\|\|** OR operator will return **FALSE**. This is useful in PHP scripts to perform a certain action if either one of two test conditions has been met.

The third logical **!** NOT operator is a "unary" operator – that is used before a single operand. It returns the inverse value of the given operand, so if the variable **$var** is a **TRUE** value then **! $var** would return a **FALSE** value. The **!** NOT operator is useful in PHP scripts to toggle the value of a variable in successive loop iterations with a statement like **$var = ! $var**. This ensures that on each pass the value is reversed, like flicking a light switch on and off.

Hot tip

The term "Boolean" refers to a system of logical thought developed by the English mathematician George Boole (1815-1864).

1 Create a valid HTML document, like the one listed on page 16, then insert PHP tags into the body section
```php
<?php
  # Statements to be inserted here.
?>
```

logic.php

2 Now, insert between the PHP tags statements to create and initialize two variables
```php
$yes = TRUE ; $no = FALSE ;
```

Hot tip

PHP also has an **XOR** (exclusive **OR**) operator that performs the equivalent evaluation of **AND NOT** together.

3 Next, insert statements to display AND evaluations
```php
$result = ( $no && $no ) ? 'TRUE' : 'FALSE' ;
        echo "No AND No returns $result <br>" ;
$result = ( $yes && $no ) ? 'TRUE' : 'FALSE' ;
        echo "Yes AND No returns : $result <br>" ;
$result = ( $yes && $yes ) ? 'TRUE' : 'FALSE' ;
        echo "Yes AND Yes returns $result <hr>" ;
```

4 Insert statements to display OR and NOT evaluations
```php
$result = ( $no || $no ) ? 'TRUE' : 'FALSE' ;
        echo "No OR No returns $result <br>" ;
$result = ( $yes || $no ) ? 'TRUE' : 'FALSE' ;
        echo "Yes OR No returns $result <br>" ;
$result = ( $yes || $yes ) ? 'TRUE' : 'FALSE' ;
        echo "Yes OR Yes returns $result <hr>" ;
$result = ( ! $yes ) ? 'TRUE' : 'FALSE' ;
        echo "NOT Yes returns $result <br>" ;
```

41

5 Save the document in your web browser's **/htdocs** directory as **logic.php** then open the page via HTTP to see the results get displayed

Don't forget

Notice that evaluation of **FALSE && FALSE** returns **FALSE** – demonstrating the anecdote "two wrongs don't make a right".

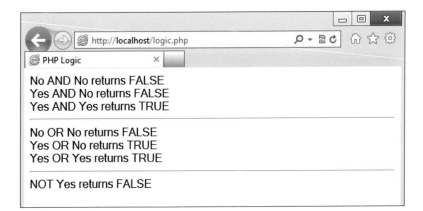

```
http://localhost/logic.php
PHP Logic

No AND No returns FALSE
Yes AND No returns FALSE
Yes AND Yes returns TRUE

No OR No returns FALSE
Yes OR No returns TRUE
Yes OR Yes returns TRUE

NOT Yes returns FALSE
```

Defining constants

Where a script is required to use a fixed data value that will never change it should be stored in a PHP "constant" rather than in a variable. A constant is a named container in a PHP script in which a data value can be stored and can be referenced using the constant's name. Unlike a variable the stored value cannot be changed as the script proceeds. This safeguards the constant value from accidental alteration and is good programming practice.

Constant names are subject to the same naming conventions as variable names, described on page 26, but it is traditional to use uppercase characters for constant names – to easily distinguish them from variable names when reading the source code. More significantly, constant names are not prefixed by a $ dollar sign.

PHP constants are not created in the same way as PHP variables. Instead, you must use a **define()** function to specify the constant's name and the value it will contain, with this syntax:

define('NAME' , value) ;

A constant can only contain alphanumeric values (character strings, integer and floating-point numbers) so they may not contain Boolean values of **TRUE** or **FALSE**, nor represent an object or a **NULL** empty value.

Although constant values can be accessed just like variable values, using their name to reference the value they contain, constants cannot be included in mixed strings for display – as the PHP interpreter cannot distinguish a constant name from a regular capitalized string of text. For example:

define('USER' , 'Mike') ;
echo "Hello USER" ; **# Displays: Hello USER**

So the constant value must be referenced separately with

echo 'Hello ' ;
echo USER ;

or by concatenating the referenced value to the string like this:

echo 'Hello ' . USER ;

Constants defined by the script author can be used just like the predefined constants that are built into PHP such as **PHP_VERSION** and **PHP_OS** that describe the version and server operating system.

Hot tip

When creating a variable always consider whether its value will ever change – if not you should create a constant instead. For example, **define('PI' , 3.14) ;**

1 Create a valid HTML document, like the one listed on page 16, then insert PHP tags into the body section

```
<?php
    # Statements to be inserted here.
?>
```

constant.php

2 Now, insert between the PHP tags a statement to create and initialize a constant

```
define( 'USER' , 'Mike' ) ;
```

3 Next, insert a statement to display the constant value in a concatenated string

```
echo '<p>Hello ' . USER . '</p>' ;
```

4 Insert a statement to display the predefined constant value of the PHP version in a concatenated string

```
echo '<p>You are using PHP version ' . PHP_VERSION ;
```

5 Finally, insert a statement to display the predefined constant value of the host operating system in a string

```
echo ' running on ' . PHP_OS . '</p>' ;
```

6 Save the document in your web browser's **/htdocs** directory as **constant.php** then open the page via HTTP to see the results get displayed

Beware

You cannot include constants in mixed strings or change their value or begin their name with a dollar sign.

Don't forget

You should always use uppercase for constant names to easily differentiate them from variables in your code.

43

Summary

- In PHP a variable is a named container in which a <u>changeable</u> data value can be stored and a constant is a named container in which a <u>fixed</u> data value can be stored

- The value stored in a variable or in a constant can be referenced using its name

- Variable names must begin with a **$** dollar sign, may comprise letters, numbers, and underscore characters, and the first character after the **$** must only be a letter or an underscore

- Constant names are not prefixed by a **$** and are all uppercase

- A variable is initialized using the = assignment operator, whereas a constant is initialized using the **define()** function

- A variable's value can be displayed as part of a mixed string by enclosing the string and variable name in double quotes only

- Strings may be enclosed in either single quotes or double quotes and inner quote marks can be escaped using a backslash

- String values can be joined together into a single string using the . period concatenation operator

- An array variable can store multiple items of data in sequential array elements that are numbered starting at zero by default

- Optionally, key names may be specified for each array element

- A **foreach** loop can be used to access each element in an array

- The **implode()** and **explode()** functions convert between strings and arrays by adding or removing specified separators

- Arrays can be sorted into alphanumeric order by value or key

- A multi-dimensional array is simply an array whose elements are themselves arrays

- PHP has operators to perform arithmetic (**+ - * / % ++ --**) , comparison (**== != > < >= <= ?:**) , and logic (**&& || !**)

3 Controlling progress

This chapter demonstrates how to make PHP statements that evaluate expressions to determine how a script should proceed.

Branching alternatives

The **if** keyword is used to perform the basic conditional test that evaluates a given expression for a Boolean value of **TRUE** or **FALSE**. Statements within braces following the evaluation will only be executed when the expression is found to be **TRUE**. So the syntax of an **if** test statement looks like this:

if (*test-expression*) { *statements-to-execute-when-true* }

There may be multiple statements to be executed when the test is **TRUE** but each statement must be terminated by a semi-colon.

Multiple expressions can be tested using the logical **&&** AND operator to ensures that following statements will only be executed when both expressions are found to be **TRUE**, like this:

if ((*test-expression*) && (*test-expression*))
 { *statements-to-execute-when-true* }

It is often preferable to extend an **if** statement by appending an **else** statement specifying statements within braces to be executed when the expessions evaluated by the **if** statement are found to be **FALSE**, with this syntax:

if (*test-expression*)
 { *statements-to-execute-when-true* }
else
 { *statements-to-execute-when-false* }

Alternative expressions may also be evaluated in a conditional test by adding an **elseif** statement specifying statements within braces to be executed when the alternative expession is found to be **TRUE**. An **else** statement can be appended here too to specify statements within braces to be executed when the expessions evaluated by the **if** and **elseif** statements are found to be **FALSE**, with this syntax:

if (*test-expression*)
 { *statements-to-execute-when-true* }

elseif (*test-expression*)
 { *statements-to-execute-when-alternative-is-true* }
else
 { *statements-to-execute-when-all-expressions-are-false* }

This is a fundamental programming technique that offers the script different directions in which to proceed, depending on the result of the evaluations, and is known as "conditional branching".

46

Hot tip

When the code to be executed is just a single statement the braces may optionally be omitted.

Hot tip

The **elseif** keyword can also be written as two separate words **else if**.

1 Begin a PHP script with a statement that outputs a result only when a tested expression is found to be **TRUE**

```php
<?php

if ( 4 > 2 ) { echo '<p>Yes, 4 is greater than 2 <br>' ; }
```

ifelse.php

2 Next, add a statement that outputs a result only when two tested expressions are both found to be **TRUE**

```php
if ( ( 4 > 2 ) && ( 8 > 4 ) )
{ echo '4 is greater than 2 AND 8 is greater than 4<br>' ; }
```

3 Now, add a statement that outputs a result when a tested expression is found to be **TRUE** or **FALSE**

```php
if ( 4 > 8 )
{ echo '4 is greater than 8 <br>' ; }
else
{ echo '4 is less than 8 <br>' ; }
```

4 Finally, add a statement that outputs a result when either of two tested expressions are found to be **TRUE** or when both tested expressions are found to be **FALSE**

```php
if ( 4 > 8 )
{ echo 'This test is True </p>' ; }
elseif ( 8 > 4 )
{ echo 'Alternative test is True </p>' ; }
else
{ echo 'Both tests are False </p>' ; }          ?>
```

5 Save the document in your web browser's **/htdocs** directory as **ifelse.php** then open the page via HTTP to see the results of conditional branching get displayed

Hot tip

You can nest conditional if tests (one inside another) so that statements in the inner block only get executed when both tests are found to be **TRUE**.

47

Switching branches

Conditional branching performed by multiple **if-elseif-else** statements can often be performed more efficiently by a **switch** statement when the test expression just evaluates one condition.

 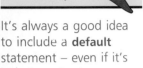
The **switch** statement works in an unusual way. It takes a given value as its parameter argument then seeks to match that value from a number of **case** statements. Code to be executed when a match is found is included in each **case** statement.

It is important to end each **case** statement with a **break** keyword statement so the **switch** statement will then exit when a match is found without seeking further matches – unless that is the deliberate requirement.

Optionally, the list of **case** statements can be followed by a single final **default** statement to specify code to be executed in the event that no matches are found within any of the **case** statements. So the syntax of a switch statement typically looks like this:

```
switch ( test-value )
{
    case match-value : statements-to-execute-when-matched ; break ;
    case match-value : statements-to-execute-when-matched ; break ;
    case match-value : statements-to-execute-when-matched ; break ;
    default : statements-to-execute-when-no-match-found ;
}
```

A **switch** statement can have many **case** statements but no two of its **case** statements can attempt to match the same value.

Where a number of match-values are to each execute the same statements only the final **case** statement need include the statements to be executed and the **break** statement to exit the **switch** statement block. For example, to output the same message for match-values of 0, 1, and 2:

```
switch ( $number )
{
    case 0 :
    case 1 :
    case 2 : echo 'Less than 3' ; break ;
    case 3 : echo 'Exactly 3' ; break ;
    default : echo 'Greater than 3 or less than zero' ;
}
```

① Begin a PHP script with statements that create and initialize two variables with an integer and character value
`$number = 2 ; $letter = 'B' ;`

switch.php

② Next, add a **switch** statement that attempts to match the integer value

```
switch ( $number )
{
  case 1 : echo 'Number is One<br>' ; break ;
  case 2 : echo 'Number is Two<br>' ; break ;
  case 3 : echo 'Number is Three<br>' ; break ;
  default : echo 'Number is Unrecognized<br>' ;
}
```

③ Now, add a **switch** statement that attempts to match the character value

```
switch ( $letter )
{
  case 'A' : echo 'Letter is A<br>' ; break ;
  case 'B' : echo 'Letter is B<br>' ; break ;
  case 'C' : echo 'Letter is C<br>' ; break ;
  default : echo 'Letter is Unrecognized<br>' ;
}
```

④ Finally, add a **switch** statement to attempt to match against multiple integer values

```
switch ( $number )
{
  case 0 : case 1 : case 2 : echo 'Less than 3<br>' ; break ;
  default : echo '3 or more, or less than zero' ;
}
```

Hot tip

In **switch** statements the **case** keyword, match-value, and colon character are regarded as a unique "label".

⑤ Save the document in your web browser's **/htdocs** directory as **switch.php** then open the page via HTTP to see the results of conditional branching get displayed

Performing loops

A loop is a piece of code in a script that automatically repeats. One complete execution of all statements within a loop is called an "iteration", or a "pass". The length of a loop is controlled by a conditional test made within the loop. While the tested expression is found to be **TRUE** the loop will continue – until the tested expression is found to be **FALSE** at which point the loop ends.

In PHP there are these four types of loop structure:

- **for** loop – performs a specified number of iterations

- **while** loop – performs iterations only while a test made at the start of each iteration evaluates as **TRUE**

- **do while** loop – performs iterations only while a test made at the end of each iteration evaluates as **TRUE**

- **foreach** loop – performs iterations through each element of an array, as introduced on page 30

Perhaps the most interesting loop structure is the **for** loop, which typically has this syntax:

```
for ( initializer ; test-expression ; incrementer )
{ statements-to-be-executed }
```

The initializer is used to set a starting value for a counter of the number of iterations made by the loop. An integer variable is used for this purpose and is traditionally named "i".

Upon each iteration of the loop the test-expression is evaluated and that iteration will only continue while this expression is **TRUE**. When the test-expression becomes **FALSE** the loop ends immediately without executing the statements again. With every iteration the counter is incremented then the statements executed.

Loops can be nested, one within another, to allow complete execution of all iterations of an inner nested loop on each iteration of the outer loop.

1 Begin a PHP script with a **for** loop to output the loop counter value in a list on each of three iterations

```
for ( $i = 1 ; $i < 4 ; $i++ )
{
  echo "<dt>Outer loop iteration $i" ;

  # Nested loop to be inserted here.
}
```

forloop.php

2 Save the document in your web browser's **/htdocs** directory as **forloop.php** then open the page via HTTP to see the loop counter values get displayed

3 Now, insert a nested **for** loop to output its loop counter value in a list on each of three iterations

```
for ( $j = 1 ; $j < 4 ; $j++ )
{
  echo "<dd>Inner loop iteration $j" ;
}
```

4 Save the document once more then open the page via HTTP to see both loop counter values get displayed

51

Hot tip

A **for** loop counter can also count down – by decrementing the counter value on each iteration using **i--** instead of **i++**.

Looping while true

A **while** loop is an alternative to the **for** loop described in the previous example. The **while** loop also requires an initializer, test-expression, and an incrementer, but these are not neatly listed within a single pair of parentheses as they are in a **for** loop. Instead, the initializer must appear before the start of the loop block, the test-expression must appear within parentheses after the **while** keyword, followed by braces containing both an incrementer and the statements to be executed on each iteration:

```
initializer
while ( test-expression )
{ statements-to-be-executed ; incrementer }
```

A **do while** loop provides a subtle variation on the syntax above by placing the **do** keyword before the loop block and moving the **while** statement to after the loop block:

```
initializer
do { statements-to-be-executed ; incrementer }
while ( test-expression ) ;
```

Both **while** loops and **do while** loops will proceed to make iterations until the test-expression is found to be **FALSE**, at which point the loop will exit. It is therefore essential that the loop body contains code that will, at some point, change the result of the test-expression evaluation – otherwise an infinite loop is created that will lock the system.

The significant difference between a **while** loop and a **do while** loop is that a **while** loop will not make a single iteration if the test-expression is **FALSE** on its first evaluation. In contrast, a **do while** loop will always make at least one iteration because its statements are executed before the evaluation is made. If this is desirable a **do while** loop is obviously the best choice, otherwise the choice between a **for** loop and a **while** loop is largely a matter of personal preference. One rule of thumb suggests that a **for** loop is best used to perform a specific number of iterations, whereas a **while** loop is best used to iterate until a certain condition is met.

Loops are the perfect partner to use with arrays as each iteration can effortlessly read or write into successive array elements.

① Begin a PHP script with a statement to create an array
`$numbers = array(10 , 20 , 30) ;`

whileloop.php

② Next, add a **while** loop to output the value of each array element

```
echo '<dt>While Loop : ' ;
$i = 0 ;
while ( $i < 3 )
{
  echo "<dd>Element $i = $numbers[$i] " ;
  $i++ ;
}
```

③ Now, add a **do while** loop to output the value of each array element

```
echo '<dt>Do While Loop : ' ;
$i = 0 ;
do
{
  echo "<dd>Element $i = $numbers[$i] " ;
  $i++ ;
}
while ( $i < 3 ) ;
```

④ Save the document in your web browser's **/htdocs** directory as **whileloop.php** then open the page via HTTP to see the array element values get identically displayed

Don't forget

Change the value in this test expression to zero so **while ($i = 0)** in both loops to see only the first iteration of the **do while** loop get executed.

53

Breaking from loops

The **break** keyword can be used to prematurely terminate a loop when a specified condition is met. The **break** statement is situated inside the loop statement block and is preceded by a test expression. When the test returns **TRUE** the loop ends immediately and the program proceeds on to the next task. For example, in a nested inner loop it proceeds to the next iteration of the outer loop.

breakcontinue.php

1 Begin a PHP script with a **for** loop that performs three iterations
```
for ( $i = 1 ; $i < 4 ; $i++ )
{
    # Nested loop to be inserted here (step 2).
}
```

2 Next, insert a nested **for** loop that also performs three iterations
```
for ( $j = 1 ; $j < 4 ; $j++ )
{
    # Statements to be inserted here (steps 5 & 6).
}
```

3 Now, insert a statement that outputs the value of both loop counters on each iteration
```
echo "Running i = $i and j = $j <br>" ;
```

4 Save the document in your web browser's **/htdocs** directory as **breakcontinue.php** then open the page via HTTP to see both loop counter values get displayed

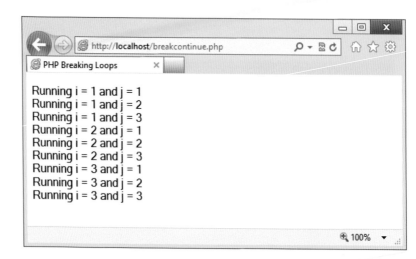

5 Next, insert this **break** statement at the very beginning of the inner loop block, to break out of the inner loop – then save the document and view the change

```php
if ( $i == 2 && $j == 1 )
{
  echo "Breaks inner loop when i = $i and j = $j <br>" ;
  break ;
}
```

Don't forget

Here the **break** statement halts all three iterations of the inner loop when the outer loop tries to run it the second time.

```
http://localhost/breakcontinue.php
PHP Breaking Loops

Running i = 1 and j = 1
Running i = 1 and j = 2
Running i = 1 and j = 3
Breaks inner loop when i = 2 and j = 1
Running i = 3 and j = 1
Running i = 3 and j = 2
Running i = 3 and j = 3
```

The **continue** keyword can be used to skip a single iteration of a loop when a specified condition is met. The **continue** statement is situated inside the loop statement block and is preceded by a test expression. When the test returns **TRUE** that single iteration ends.

6 Now, insert this **continue** statement at the beginning of the inner loop block, to skip the first iteration of the inner loop – then save the document then view the change

```php
if ( $i == 1 && $j == 1 )
{
  echo "Continues inner loop when i = $i and j = $j <br>" ;
  continue ;
}
```

Don't forget

Here the **continue** statement just skips the first iteration of the inner loop when the outer loop tries to run it for the first time.

```
http://localhost/breakcontinue.php
PHP Breaking Loops

Continues inner loop when i = 1 and j = 1
Running i = 1 and j = 2
Running i = 1 and j = 3
Breaks inner loop when i = 2 and j = 1
Running i = 3 and j = 1
Running i = 3 and j = 2
Running i = 3 and j = 3
```

Creating functions

PHP provides many built-in functions that can be called by name in your scripts to execute pre-defined actions, such as the array sorting functions described on page 32. Additionally, you may create your own custom functions to execute specified actions when called. This usefully allows PHP scripts to be modularized into sections of code that are easier to understand and maintain.

Your custom function names may contain any combination of letters, numbers, and the underscore character, but must begin with a letter or an underscore. Understandably, the name may not duplicate an existing built-in function name to avoid conflict, so for example you may not create a custom function named "sort".

As with PHP variables, function names are case-sensitive so **cube()**, **Cube()**, and **CUBE()** call three separate individual functions.

A function is created in a PHP script simply by stating its name, after the **function** keyword, followed by parentheses and curly brackets (braces) containing the statements to be executed each time that function gets called:

```
function function_name ( )
{
    statements-to-be-executed
}
```

When creating custom functions it is important to understand how variable accessibility is limited by the variable's "scope":

Beware

Always avoid using the **global** keyword to alter the scope of local variables to maintain your code integrity.

- Variables created outside a function have "global" scope but are not accessible from within any function block

- Variables created inside a function have "local" scope so are only accessible from within that particular function block

As a variable created within a function is not accessible from elsewhere its name may duplicate the name of a variable outside a function block, or within another function block, without conflict. This allows a global variable to contain a different value to local variables of the same name.

The scope of a variable created within a function can be altered to make it available globally by preceding its declaration with the **global** keyword – but this is bad practice and should be avoided.

function.php

① Begin a PHP script with a statement to create and initialize a global variable

```
$result = 5 + 5 ;
```

② Next, add a **function** to create and initialize a local variable of the same name, and to output its value

```
function square()
{
  $result = 5 * 5 ;
  echo "Local Square Result = $result<br>" ;
}
```

③ Now, add another **function** to create and initialize a local variable of the same name again, and to output its value

```
function cube()
{
  $result = 5 * 5 * 5 ;
  echo "Local Cube Result = $result<br>" ;
}
```

④ Finally, add statements to output the value of the global variable and call both custom functions

```
echo "Global Sum Result = $result<br>" ;
square() ;
cube() ;
```

⑤ Save the document in your web browser's **/htdocs** directory as **function.php** then open the page via HTTP to see the like-named variable values get displayed

http://localhost/function.php

PHP Functions

Global Sum Result = 10
Local Square Result = 25
Local Cube Result = 125

🔍 100%

Don't forget

Variables of the same name do not conflict when they are declared in a different scope – they are not visible to each other.

Passing arguments

Data can be passed to custom functions as "arguments" (also known as "parameters") in the same way you can pass arguments to some built-in PHP functions. For example the **sort()** function takes the array to be sorted as its argument.

Functions can be created with any number of arguments but when called data must be supplied for each argument to avoid an error.

A function containing arguments is created by including a comma-separated list of argument variables within the parentheses after the function name like this:

```
function function_name ( $arg_1 , $arg_2 , $arg_3 )
{
    statements-to-be-executed
}
```

Argument names must adhere to the same naming conventions required for other PHP variables and should ideally be meaningful to represent the nature of the data they will be passed. The argument data must be passed by the call in the correct order and can then be used by the statements within that function:

```
function print_name( $first_name , $last_name )
{
    echo "Name is $first_name $last_name " ;
}
```

```
print_name( 'Mickey' , 'Mouse' ) ;        # Name is Mickey Mouse
```

The function call may pass literal values, like the strings in the example above, or may pass regular variables – which in turn supply their values to the function. For instance:

```
$forename = 'Donald' ;
$surname = 'Duck' ;
print_name( $forename , $surname ) ;    # Name is Donald Duck
```

Argument variables have local scope so are only accessible within the function in which they are created. This means the same argument names may be used in many functions without conflict with each other or with regular variable names.

Don't forget

Arguments must be specified in the function declaration and passed by the caller as a comma-separated list.

1 Begin a PHP script with a statement to create and initialize a global variable

```
$number = 5 ;
```

argument.php

2 Next, add a **function** with one argument to utilize its value in a calculation and to output its result

```
function square( $number )
{
  $result = $number * $number ;
  echo "$number Squared = $result<br>" ;
}
```

3 Now, add another **function** with one argument to utilize its value in a calculation and to output its result

```
function cube( $number )
{
  $result = $number * $number * $number ;
  echo "$number Cubed = $result<br>" ;
}
```

4 Finally, add statements to call the functions passing both literal and variable arguments

```
square( 3 ) ;
cube( 4 ) ;
square( $number ) ;
cube( $number ) ;
```

5 Save the document in your web browser's **/htdocs** directory as **argument.php** then open the page via HTTP to see the results get displayed

Hot tip

You can use the same name for the argument and a regular variable to be passed to it for easy recognition.

59

Returning values

Some PHP functions return values when called and the nature of the returned value may be determined by the argument passed. For example, the built-in **date()** function accepts a whole range of arguments to determine how date information should be formatted for return to the caller:

Argument:	Description:	Example:
Y	Year as four digits	2014
y	Year as two digits	14
n	Month as one or two digits	7
m	Month as two digits	07
F	Month full name	February
M	Month name as three letters	Feb
j	Day as one or two digits	4
d	Day as two digits	04
l	Weekday full name	Monday
D	Weekday as three letters	Mon
S	Ordinal suffix as two letters	th
H	Hour in 24-hour format	14
i	Minutes	45
s	Seconds	30

Hot tip

These are just some of the possible **date()** function arguments – you can discover the complete range in the PHP manual online at **php.net/manual**.

Your own custom functions can also be made to return a value when called simply by using the **return** keyword in a statement followed by the value that is to be returned. Typically, this will be the final statement in the function's statement block.

1. Begin a PHP script with statements to set the timezone and initialize a global variable with a user name

```php
date_default_timezone_set( 'UTC' ) ;
$user = ' Mike' ;
```

return.php

2. Next, add a function with no arguments to return the weekday, day with suffix, and month name when called

```php
function display_date( )
{
  return date( 'l, jS F' ) ;
}
```

3. Now, add a function with one argument to return an appropriate user greeting for the current time of day

```php
function welcome( $user )
{
  $hour = date( 'H' ) ;
  $greeting = ( $hour < 12 ) ?
        '<br>Good Morning' : '<br>Good Day' ;
  $greeting .= $user ;
  return $greeting ;
}
```

4. Finally, add statements to call the functions passing the global variable as an argument

```php
echo display_date() ;
echo welcome( $user ) ;
```

5. Save the document in your web browser's **/htdocs** directory as **return.php** then open the page via HTTP to see the returns get displayed

Don't forget

The default timezone must be set to use the **date()** function – either in the PHP configuration file or with the **date_default_timezone_set()** function as seen here.

61

Summary

- The **if** keyword performs the basic conditional test that evaluates an expression for a Boolean value of **TRUE** or **FALSE**

- An **else** statement specifies statements to be executed when the expessions evaluated by the **if** statement are found to be **FALSE**

- Alternative expressions may be evaluated in a conditional test by adding an **elseif** statement

- Multiple **if-elseif-else** statements can often be performed more efficiently by a **switch** statement

- Each **case** statement must end with a **break** keyword statement so the **switch** statement will exit when a match is found

- A **default** statement specifies code to be executed in the event that no matches are found within any **case** statements

- A loop is a piece of code in a script that automatically repeats until a test expression becomes **FALSE**

- The PHP loop structures are **for, while, do while,** and **foreach**

- The **break** keyword can be used to prematurely terminate a loop when a specified condition is met

- The **continue** keyword can be used to skip a single iteration of a loop when a specified condition is met

- Functions execute specified actions when called and allow scripts to be modularized into sections of code

- A function is created by stating its name after the **function** keyword followed by parentheses and curly brackets

- A comma-separated list of arguments can be included within the parentheses after a function name

- Functions can return a value when called by using the **return** keyword in a statement followed by the value to be returned

4 Producing forms

This chapter demonstrates how to use PHP scripts to process HTML form data.

Performing actions

Processing data submitted from an HTML form on a web page is perhaps the most fundamental task performed by a PHP script.

The HTML **<form>** tag's **action** attribute is used to nominate the PHP script that will process ("handle") the form data. Additionally, the **<form>** tag's **method** attribute is used to specify how the data is sent to the script – typically by the **POST** method. So the HTML form tag and attributes might look like this:

```
<form action="script.php" method="POST">
```

PHP provides a special "superglobal" **$_POST** array variable in which it stores form data submitted by the **POST** method. It creates an array element of the same name as each submitted form element name, storing the value they contain. For example, with this form element:

```
<input type="text" name="email" >
```

On submission of the form, PHP will create an array element named **$_POST['email']** containing the value entered into that form input by the user.

For easy recognition, PHP variables of the same names as the form elements can be assigned the values stored in their corresponding **$_POST** array elements. The values can then be displayed in a response page created by the action handler script.

action.php

① Create an HTML document containing a form with three text input fields for data submission
```
<form action="action_handler.php" method="POST">
<dl>
<dt>Name:
<dd><input type="text" name="name">
<dt>Email Address:
<dd><input type="text" name="mail">
<dt>Comments:
<dd><textarea rows="5" cols="20" name="comment" >
</textarea>
</dl>
<p><input type="submit" ></p>
</form>
```

② Now, save the document in your web browser's **/htdocs** directory as **action.php**

3 Next, create an HTML document containing a script to assign form values to like-named PHP variables for output

```php
<?php
$name = $_POST['name'] ;
$mail = $_POST['mail'] ;
$comment = $_POST['comment'] ;
echo "<p>Thanks for this comment $name ...</p>" ;
echo "<p><i>$comment</i></p>" ;
echo "<p>We will reply to $mail</p>" ;
?>
```

action_handler.php

4 Save the document in your web browser's **/htdocs** directory as **action_handler.php** then open **action.php** via HTTP and submit some data to see it get displayed in the response page produced by the PHP script

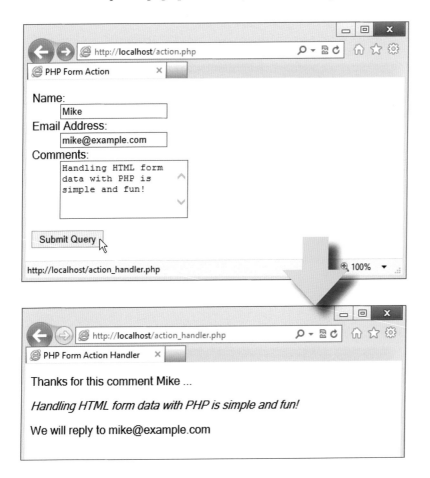

Checking set values

PHP can easily ensure that the user has entered data into submitted HTML form fields using the built-in **isset()** function. This function takes the name of a variable as its argument and returns **TRUE** only if that variable value is not **NULL** – thus ensuring that the variable has been "set" with some value. Empty form fields will be **NULL** unless the user has entered a value.

Conditional tests can be made with the **isset()** function to indicate where form fields have been left empty or to provide a response page where the fields have been completed.

isset.php

1 Create an HTML document containing a form with three radio buttons providing a single field for data submission

```
<form action="isset_handler.php" method="POST">
<fieldset>
<legend>What kind of language is PHP?</legend>
Scripting<input type="radio"
        name="definition" value="Scripting"> <br>
Markup<input type="radio"
        name="definition" value="Markup"> <br>
Programming<input type="radio"
        name="definition" value="Programming">
</fieldset><p><input type="submit" ></p>
</form>
```

2 Now, save the document in your web browser's **/htdocs** directory as **isset.php**

isset_handler.php

3 Next, create an HTML document containing a PHP script to initialize a variable with a submitted value – or with **NULL** if no value has been submitted

```
<?php

if ( isset( $_POST['definition'] ) )
{
  $definition = $_POST['definition'] ;
}
else
{
  $definition = NULL ;
}

# Response statements to be inserted here.

?>
```

4 Finally, insert statements to output an appropriate
 response according to the value of the variable

```
if ( $definition != NULL )
{
  if ( $definition != 'Scripting' )
  { echo "$definition is Incorrect" ; }
  else
  { echo "$definition is Correct" ; }
}
else
{ echo 'You must select one answer' ; }
```

Hot tip

It is technically more
efficient to test whether
a condition is not **TRUE**
than whether it is **TRUE**
– as fewer possibilities
need evaluating.

5 Save the document in your web browser's **/htdocs**
 directory as **isset_handler.php** then open **isset.php** via
 HTTP and submit the form to see the responses

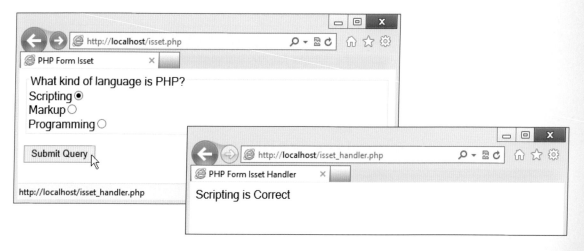

Validating form data

As users may inadvertently submit forms with empty fields or with data in the wrong format it is essential your PHP scripts ensure required fields are completed and submitted data is valid.

To ensure the user has entered something into a text field, PHP provides an **empty()** function that accepts a variable argument and returns **TRUE** if its value is an empty string, zero, **NULL** or **FALSE**.

To ensure the user has entered data in numeric format, PHP provides an **is_numeric()** function that accepts a variable argument and returns **TRUE** only if its value is a number.

More specific data validation can be performed using the PHP **preg_match()** function that accepts a "regular expression" argument and a variable argument in which to seek a pattern. Typically, this is used to ensure an email address is in the expected format.

valid.php

1. Create an HTML document containing a form with two text fields for data submission
```
<form action="valid_handler.php" method="POST">
<fieldset>
<legend>Enter a quantity and email address</legend>
<p>Quantity : <input type="text" name="quantity"></p>
<p>Email Address : <input type="text" name="email"></p>
</fieldset><p><input type="submit" ></p>
</form>
```

2. Now, save the document in your web browser's **/htdocs** directory as **valid.php**

valid_handler.php

3. Next, create an HTML document containing a PHP script to initialize a variable with a submitted value – or with **NULL** if no value has been submitted
```
if ( !empty ( $_POST['quantity'] ) )
{
  $quantity = $_POST['quantity'] ;
  # Format validation to be inserted here.
}
else
{ $quantity = NULL ; echo 'You must enter a quantity<br>' ; }
```

4. Insert statements to ensure the format is numeric
```
if ( !is_numeric( $quantity ) )
{ $quantity = NULL ; echo 'Quantity must be numeric<br>' ; }
```

⑤ Now, add statements to initialize another variable with a
submitted value – or with **NULL** if no value is submitted

```
if ( !empty ( $_POST['email'] ) )
{
  $email = $_POST['email'] ;
  # Format validation to be inserted here.
}
else
{ $email = NULL ; echo 'You must enter an email address' ; }
```

⑥ Next, insert statements to ensure email address uses the
expected pattern

```
$pattern = '/\b[\w.-]+@[\w.-]+\.[A-Za-z]{2,6}\b/' ;
if ( !preg_match( $pattern , $email ) )
{ $email = NULL ; echo 'Email address is incorrect format' ; }
```

⑦ Finally, add a statement to output valid submitted data

```
if ( ( $quantity != NULL ) && ( $email != NULL ) )
{ echo "Email : $email<br>Quantity : $quantity " ; }
```

⑧ Save the document in your web browser's **/htdocs**
directory as **valid_handler.php** then open **valid.php** via
HTTP and submit the form to see the responses

Hot tip

Strictly speaking,
the topic of regular
expressions is outside
the remit of this book
but you can precisely
copy the pattern in this
example to ensure email
addresses are in the
expected format.

69

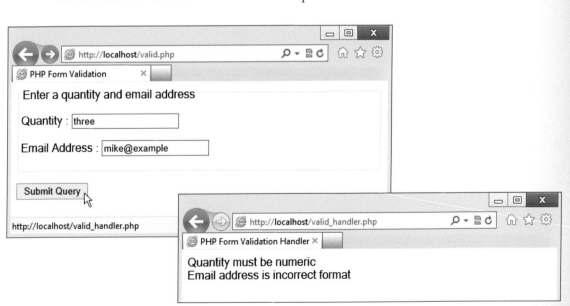

Sending hidden data

In addition to data entered by the user into HTML form input fields, data generated by PHP can be submitted using HTML form hidden fields. Like regular input fields these also send a name=value pair to the form handler script but here the value is supplied by PHP, not by the user.

Typically, data submitted using hidden form fields might include the login name of the user and a timestamp of the submission.

hidden.php

1. Create an HTML document containing a PHP script to define the timezone and initialize two variables

```
date_default_timezone_set( 'UTC' ) ;
$time = date( ' H:i , F j ' ) ;
$user = 'Mike' ;
```

2. Now, add a statement to write a complete form containing a regular input field and two hidden fields whose values are set by the variables

```
echo '
<form action="hidden_handler.php" method="POST">
<fieldset>
<legend>Send us your comments</legend>
<textarea rows="5" cols="20" name="comment">
</textarea>
<input type="hidden" name="user" value=" '. $user .' ">
<input type="hidden" name="time" value=" '. $time.' ">
</fieldset><p><input type="submit" ></p></form> ' ;
```

3. Save the document in your web browser's **/htdocs** directory as **hidden.php**

hidden_handler.php

4. Next, create an HTML document containing a PHP script to initialize a variable with a submitted value – or with **NULL** if no value has been submitted

```
if ( !empty ( $_POST['comment'] ) )
{
  $comment = $_POST['comment'] ;
}
else
{
  $comment = NULL ;
  echo 'You must enter a comment' ;
}
```

5 Now, add statements to initialize two variables if the hidden form field values have been set
```
$time =
( !isset ( $_POST['time'] ) ) ? NULL : $_POST['time'] ;

$user =
( !isset ( $_POST['user'] ) ) ? NULL : $_POST['user'] ;
```

6 Finally, add a statement to output valid submitted data
```
if ( ( $comment != NULL ) &&
                ( $time != NULL ) && ( $user != NULL ) )
{ echo "<p>Comment received : \" $comment \"<br>
                        From $user at $time </p>" ; }
```

7 Save the document in your web browser's **/htdocs** directory as **hidden_handler.php** then open **hidden.php** via HTTP and submit the form to see the responses

71

Hot tip

Notice the ternary **? :** operator is used here in place of a more lengthy **if else** statement.

Don't forget

You can include quotes in output by prefixing them with a backslash to escape them from recognition – as demonstrated here.

Handling submissions

The examples so far in this chapter have each used two documents – one to display an HTML form and another to handle the form submission. This procedure can, however, be performed by a single document using a simple technique to determine whether a form should be displayed or its submission should be handled.

PHP provides a special "superglobal" **$_SERVER** array variable with a **REQUEST_METHOD** element in which it stores the type of request. Where a form uses the **POST** method for submission, two different types of request are made to the PHP script when the page loads – simply displaying the form uses the standard **GET** method made by most web pages, whereas submitting the form uses the **POST** method. Therefore the request method can be examined to determine which course of action to take.

Using this technique, the name of the same single page is also specified as the form handler to the HTML **action** attribute. The form can be displayed by the usual **echo** instruction and validation checks can be made for the response in the same way as described for separate form handler scripts.

single.php

1 Create an HTML document containing a PHP script that examines the page request method
```
if ( $_SERVER[ 'REQUEST_METHOD' ] != 'POST' )
{
    # Form display statements to be inserted here.
}
else
{
    # Form handling statements to be inserted here.
}
```

2 Now, insert a statement to display a form when the page has been requested by the standard **GET** method
```
echo '
<form action="single.php" method="POST">
<fieldset>
<legend>Send us your comments</legend>
<textarea rows="5" cols="40" name="comment">
</textarea>
</fieldset>
<p><input type="submit" ></p>
</form> ';
```

③ Next, insert a statement to handle the form submission when the page has been requested by the **POST** method

```
if ( !empty ( $_POST['comment'] ) )
{
  $comment = $_POST['comment'] ;
  echo "Comment : $comment " ;
}
else
{ $comment = NULL ; echo 'You must enter a comment' ; }
```

Hot tip

The form will be handled by the same page on submission if the action attribute specifies an empty string **action=""** – but it is preferable to specify the page name.

④ Save the document in your web browser's **/htdocs** directory as **single.php** then submit the form to see the responses

73

Making sticky forms

When a user attempts to submit a form where a required field has not been completed, it is desirable to retain the entries in the fields they have completed by making the form "sticky". This is especially so for lengthy forms with many fields so the user need not complete all fields once more and is easily achieved with PHP.

Simply assigning the relevant submitted field data from the **$_POST** array to the HTML tag's **value** attribute with **echo** retains the entry when the form is displayed again for completion. As a precaution, the statement should use the **isset()** function to check that the field was in fact completed before submission.

An error message for each incomplete field can be assigned to an array to advise of omissions when the form is displayed again, or a message written confirming success when all fields are completed.

sticky.php

1 Create an HTML document containing a sticky form with two text fields for name and email address details

```
<form action="sticky.php" method="POST">
<p>Name:
<input type="text" name="name"
        value="<?php if ( isset( $_POST['name'] ) )
                  echo $_POST['name'] ; ?>"> </p>
<p>Email:
<input type="text" name="email"
        value="<?php if ( isset( $_POST['email'] ) )
                  echo $_POST['email'] ; ?>"></p>
<p><input type="submit"></p>
</form>
```

Don't forget

The **if** statement tests that the form has been submitted by checking the request method is POST, not the GET method that is used to display the empty form.

2 Now, add a PHP script to handle the form submission

```
<?php

if ( $_SERVER[ 'REQUEST_METHOD' ] == 'POST' )
{
  # Statements to be inserted here.
}

?>
```

3 Next, insert into the PHP script block a statement to create an array for error messages

```
$errors = array() ;
```

4 Then, insert statements to initialize variables with submitted values, or add to the errors array for omissions

```
if ( empty( $_POST[ 'name' ] ) ) { $errors[] = 'name' ; }
else { $name = trim( $_POST[ 'name' ] ) ; }

if ( empty( $_POST[ 'email' ] ) ) { $errors[] = 'email' ; }
else { $email = trim( $_POST[ 'email' ] ) ; }
```

5 Now, insert statements to write error messages or confirm successful form submission

```
if( !empty( $errors ) )
{ echo 'Error! Please enter your  ' ;
  foreach ( $errors as $msg ) { echo " - $msg " ; } }
else { echo "Success! Thanks $name " ; }
```

6 Save the document in your web browser's **/htdocs** directory as **sticky.php** then open it via HTTP and submit the form to see the retained values and response messages

Hot tip

It is good practice to use the **trim()** function, as seen here, to remove any leading and trailing spaces from the submitted field value.

75

Surrounding forms

PHP usefully allows multiple files to be incorporated together to create a single web page. This means that dynamic forms can be surrounded by static header and footer content that can be easily re-used to create other pages within a website.

The PHP **include()** function takes the URL of another file to be incorporated within a web page as its argument. Typically, included static content files are HTML and are located in an "includes" folder within the **/htdocs** directory of your web server.

PHP also provides a **require()** function that works just like the **include()** function to incorporate other files within a web page but is subtly different. When the **include()** function fails, as the specified file cannot be found for example, a warning gets sent to the browser but the script continues to run. When the **require()** function fails an error is printed but the script gets halted. Usually, the **include()** function incorporates static HTML files, whereas the **require()** function incorporates dynamic PHP scripts.

Importantly, the title of a web page incorporating multiple files can be dynamically written by PHP to allow maximum flexibility of otherwise static HTML header content.

header.html

footer.html

1. Create an HTML document containing static header content and a PHP snippet to write the page title
```
<!DOCTYPE HTML>
<html lang="en">
<head>
<meta charset="UTF-8">
<title> <?php echo $page_title ; ?> </title>
<link rel="stylesheet" href="includes/style.css">
</head>

<body>
<header><h1>Page Header</h1></header>
```

2. Now, create an HTML document containing footer content
```
<footer><p>Page Footer</p></footer>
</body>
</html>
```

3. Next, create a folder named "includes" in the **/htdocs** directory of your web server and save inside it the above documents as **header.html** and **footer.html** respectively

4 Create a CSS style sheet to present the header and footer content (and rules to present aspects of later examples)

```css
header > h1 { border-bottom : 1px dashed black ;
              font-style : italic ; font-size : x-large ; }
footer > p { border-top : 1px dashed black ;
              font-style : italic ; }
table { border-spacing : 5px ; width : 530px ; }
th { color : #FFF ; background : #000 ; text-align : left ; }
td { border-bottom : 1px solid black ;
     padding : 3px ; background : #F0F0F0 ;
     text-align : left ; vertical-align :top ; }
p#err_msg { color : #F00 ; font-weight : bold ; }
```

style.css

5 Save the style sheet in the **/includes** folder you have created, alongside the HTML header and footer files

6 Finally, create a PHP script that sets the web page title and surrounds a form with header and footer content

```php
$page_title = 'PHP Include' ;
include ( 'includes/header.html' ) ;
echo '<form action="include.php" method="POST">
<p>Name: <input type="text" name="name"> </p>
<p>Email: <input type="text" name="email" ></p>
<p><input type="submit"></p></form>' ;
include ( 'includes/footer.html' ) ;
```

include.php

7 Save the PHP script in your web browser's **/htdocs** directory as **include.php** then open it via HTTP to see the page title set and a form surrounded by static content

Hot tip

You can use your browser's View Source facility to see that the entire content has been effectively incorporated into a single web page.

77

Appending link data

PHP pre-defined "superglobal" variables, such as the **$_SERVER** array variable that stores the page request method and the **$_SESSION** array variable that stores user data across pages of a website until the user quits, are accessible in all scopes of any script.

Where an HTML form submits data using the **POST** method the **$_POST** array stores the value of submitted form values in like-named array elements. So the value of a submitted field named "city" can be accessed using **$_POST['city']**.

Similarly, where data is submitted using the GET method, the **$_GET** array stores the value of submitted values in named array elements. So the value of a submitted data named "id" can be accessed using **$_GET['id']**. This is typically used to submit data to a script by appending a name=value pair to the URL in an HTML hyperlink anchor like this:

```
<a href="www.example.com/script.php?id=1">
```

The script receiving the data, nominated by the hyperlink, may then use the passed value to determine a response.

Hot tip

The **$_SESSION** superglobal will be used to store user details in the next example.

link.php

1. Create an HTML document containing a PHP script that seeks an element named "id" within the **$_GET** array
   ```
   if ( isset ( $_GET[ 'id' ] ) )
   {
      # Handler statements to be inserted here.
   }
   ```

2. Next, insert a handler statement to assign a passed value to a like-named PHP variable
   ```
   $id = $_GET[ 'id' ] ;
   ```

3. Now, insert a handler statement to output an appropriate response according to the value passed
   ```
   switch( $id )
   {
      case 1 : echo 'Cow selected<hr>' ; break ;
      case 2 : echo 'Dog selected<hr>' ; break ;
      case 3 : echo 'Goat selected<hr>' ; break ;
   }
   ```

④ Finally, add statements to display hyperlinks with appended values

```
echo '<h1>Select a buddy</h1>' ;
echo ' <p><a href="link.php?id=1">Cow</a> |' ;
echo ' <a href="link.php?id=2">Dog</a> | ' ;
echo ' <a href="link.php?id=3">Goat</a></p>' ;
```

⑤ Save the PHP script in your web browser's **/htdocs** directory as **link.php** then open it via HTTP and click the links to see the responses for the passed values

Beware

PHP also provides a **$_REQUEST** superglobal that contains the entire contents of the **$_POST** and **$_GET** arrays. This means that **$_POST['city']** is also accessible using **$_REQUEST['city']** but this should be avoided. Always use the specific array for the type of submission instead.

Don't forget

Notice that the passed name=value pair is visible in the browser address field.

Moving location

PHP provides a **header()** function that accepts an argument to specify a raw HTTP "header" to be sent to the web browser. Headers are sent from the web server before any other data and are normally not visible to the user. Most usefully, the PHP **header()** function can set the "Location" header to re-direct the browser to a new page using this syntax:

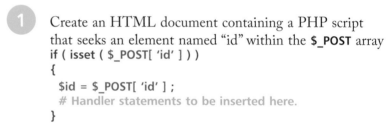

```
header( 'Location: www.example.com/page.php' ) ;
```

User data can be preserved when moving to a new page by first storing it in the special PHP superglobal **$_SESSION** array variable. This is not available automatically, however, until the **session_start()** function has been called in the script. Variable values can then be stored in like-named elements of the **$_SESSION** array so they become available from other pages on the website until the user quits or until the **session_destroy()** function is called in the script.

header.php

1 Create an HTML document containing a PHP script that seeks an element named "id" within the **$_POST** array
```
if ( isset ( $_POST[ 'id' ] ) )
{
  $id = $_POST[ 'id' ] ;
  # Handler statements to be inserted here.
}
```

2 Next, insert handler statements to store a matched id value in a **$_SESSION** array element and relocate the browser – or display a message for any other id value
```
if( $id == 123 )
{
  session_start() ;
  $_SESSION['id'] = $id ;
  header( 'Location: location.php' ) ;
  exit() ;
}
else { echo "<p>$id is an incorrect ID!</p>" ; }
```

Hot tip

It is good practice to call the **exit()** function to halt the script when relocating the browser.

3 Now, add a statement to display a form in which the user may enter an id value for submission
```
echo '<form action="header.php" method="POST">
<fieldset> <legend>Enter Your User ID</legend>
<p>ID : <input type="text" name="id"></p>
</fieldset> <input type="submit"> </form> ' ;
```

④ Save the document in your web browser's **/htdocs** directory as **header.php**

⑤ Finally, create a target HTML document containing a PHP script to display the retained **$_SESSION** array value

location.php

```
session_start() ;
if ( isset( $_SESSION['id'] ) )
{
  $id = $_SESSION['id'] ;
  echo "Welcome user ID #$id" ;
}
```

⑥ Save this document in your web browser's **/htdocs** directory as **location.php** then open **header.php** via HTTP and submit an id value to see the responses

Don't forget

Notice that the script on the target page must also call **session_start()** to make the **$_SESSION** superglobal accessible.

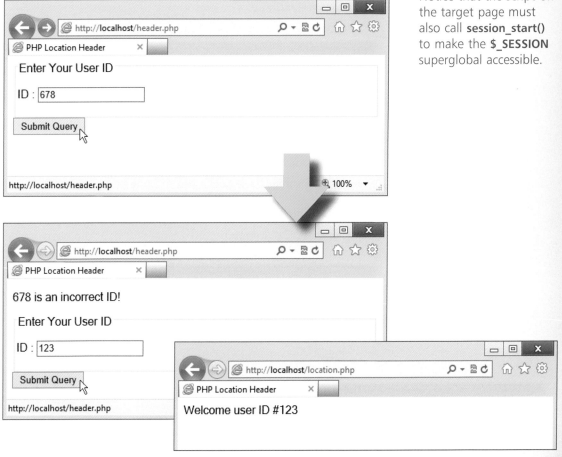

Summary

- An HTML **<form>** tag's **action** attribute specifies the PHP script to handle the form submission and its **method** attribute specifies how the data is sent to the script

- Form data submitted by the **POST** method gets automatically stored in the PHP superglobal **$_POST** array variable

- Elements of the **$_POST** array are named the same as the HTML form element containing each submitted value

- PHP can ensure that the user has entered data into submitted HTML form fields using the built-in **isset()** function

- The PHP **empty()** function checks whether a value has been entered into a form text field

- Format validation can be performed on submitted form data by the **is_numeric()** function and **preg_match()** function

- Data generated by PHP such as a timestamp created by the **date()** function can be submitted from hidden form fields

- The PHP superglobal **$_SERVER['REQUEST_METHOD']** array element stores the type of request made to load the page

- Sticky forms retain their field data simply by writing any submitted values back to the HTML input's **value** attribute

- The PHP **include()** and **require()** functions are used to incorporate other content and scripts within a web page

- Data submitted by the **GET** method gets automatically stored in the PHP superglobal **$_GET** array variable

- Hyperlinks can have name=value pairs appended to submit data to a script using the **GET** method

- A PHP script can send the browser to a new location using the **header()** function to set the HTTP Location header URL

- Data can be preserved in the PHP superglobal **$_SESSION** array variable after calling the **session_start()** function

5 Assembling tables

This chapter demonstrates how to make SQL statements that create MySQL database tables in which to store data.

Introducing tables

Databases are simply convenient storage containers that store data in a structured manner. Every database is composed of one or more tables that structure the data into organized rows and columns. This makes it easy to reference and manipulate the data.

Each database table column has a label to identify the data stored within the table cells in that column. Each row contains an entry called a "record" that places data in each cell along that row.

A typical simple database table looks like this:

```
+-----------+-------+---------+----------+----------------+
| member_id | fname | lname   | tel      | email          |
+-----------+-------+---------+----------+----------------+
|         1 | John  | Smith   | 555-1234 | john@mail.com  |
|         2 | Ann   | Jones   | 555-5678 | anne@mail.com  |
|         3 | Mike  | McGrath | 555-3456 | mike@mail.com  |
+-----------+-------+---------+----------+----------------+
```

The rows of a database table are not automatically arranged in any particular order so they can be sorted alphabetically, numerically or by any other criteria. It is important, therefore, to have some means to identify each record in the table. The example above allocates a "member_id" for this purpose and this unique identifier is known as the **PRIMARY KEY**.

Storing data in a single table is very useful but relational databases with multiple tables introduce more possibilities by allowing the stored data to be combined in a variety of ways. For instance, the following two tables could be added to the database containing the first example table shown above:

```
+----------+-------------+        +-----------+----------+
| video_id | title       |        | member_id | video_id |
+----------+-------------+        +-----------+----------+
|        1 | Titanic     |        |         1 | 3        |
|        2 | Men In Black|        |         2 | 1        |
|        3 | Star Wars   |        |         3 | 2        |
+----------+-------------+        +-----------+----------+
```

The table on the left lists several video titles sorted numerically by "video_id" number. The table on the right describes a relationship between the tables that links each member to the video they have rented. So Anne (member #2) has Titanic (video #1), John (member #1) has Star Wars (video #3) and Mike (member #3) has Men In Black (video #2).

In the MySQL Command Line Client you can display a list of all databases on your MySQL Server using this query:

SHOW DATABASES ;

To work with any database you must first tell the MySQL Server which database to use by issuing this query:

USE *database-name* ;

Once the database has been selected it is possible to view a list of all the tables it contains with this query:

SHOW TABLES ;

1. Launch the MySQL Command Line Client then enter the root password you chose during installation

2. At the **mysql>** command prompt, issue this query to list all databases that exisit on your MySQL Server
 SHOW DATABASES ;

3. Next, issue this query to use an existing database
 USE site_db ;

4. Now, issue a further query to display all tables that exist within the "site_db" database
 SHOW TABLES ;

Don't forget

You created the database named "site_db" after installation of the MySQL Server in chapter one – refer back to page 20.

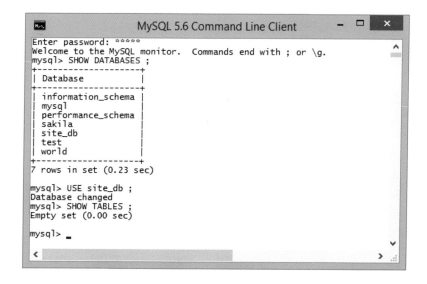

```
                    MySQL 5.6 Command Line Client         ─  □   ×
Enter password: *****
Welcome to the MySQL monitor.  Commands end with ; or \g.
mysql> SHOW DATABASES ;
+--------------------+
| Database           |
+--------------------+
| information_schema |
| mysql              |
| performance_schema |
| sakila             |
| site_db            |
| test               |
| world              |
+--------------------+
7 rows in set (0.23 sec)

mysql> USE site_db ;
Database changed
mysql> SHOW TABLES ;
Empty set (0.00 sec)

mysql> _
```

Hot tip

The **SHOW TABLES;** query in this example responds with an "empty set" message as there are no tables in the "site_db" database yet – but you will create tables there throughout the rest of this book.

Creating tables

A MySQL database table is created by issuing this query:

CREATE TABLE IF NOT EXISTS *table-name* **(** *col type , col type* **) ;**

The statement in this query must be followed by parentheses containing a comma-separated list of column definitions – defining the name of each table column and the type of data that column may contain. For example, a table named "fruit" might contain three columns named "id", "name" and "color". The **INT** keyword could specify that the "id" column may only contain integer values and the **TEXT** keyword could specify that the "name" and "color" columns may only contain text values.

You can discover the format of any table using this query:

EXPLAIN *table-name* **;**

A table may also be deleted from a database with this query:

DROP TABLE IF EXISTS *table-name* **;**

Issuing a query to create a table with many columns can be difficult to type accurately at the **mysql>** command prompt, so it is often better to create the query as an SQL text file first then implement the query using the **SOURCE** keyword at the command prompt to identify the path to the file, such as on your desktop.

Beware

You may also see shorter **CREATE TABLE** and **DROP TABLE** queries used but it is good practice to use these longer versions to check for existing tables.

create_table.sql

1. Launch a plain text editor, such as Notepad, and create a query defining the "fruit" table example described above
CREATE TABLE IF NOT EXISTS fruit
(
 id INT ,
 name TEXT ,
 color TEXT
) ;

2. Save the file on your desktop as **create_table.sql** then launch the MySQL Command Line Client and log in as a user with full access privileges, such as root

3. Next, issue a query to use the established database
USE site_db ;

4 Now, implement the SQL query by stating the source path to the SQL file on your system, such as
SOURCE C:\Users\Mike\Desktop\create_table.sql

5 Issue a query to confirm the table's existence and format
EXPLAIN fruit ;

6 Finally, delete the table and confirm its removal
DROP TABLE IF EXISTS fruit ;
SHOW TABLES ;

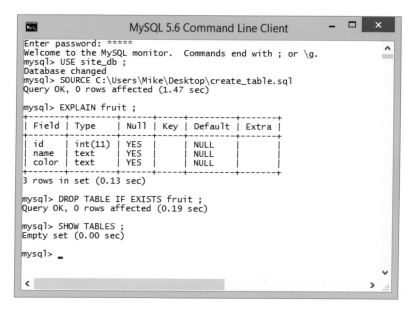

```
                    MySQL 5.6 Command Line Client          –  □  ×
Enter password: *****
Welcome to the MySQL monitor.  Commands end with ; or \g.
mysql> USE site_db ;
Database changed
mysql> SOURCE C:\Users\Mike\Desktop\create_table.sql
Query OK, 0 rows affected (1.47 sec)

mysql> EXPLAIN fruit ;
+-------+---------+------+-----+---------+-------+
| Field | Type    | Null | Key | Default | Extra |
+-------+---------+------+-----+---------+-------+
| id    | int(11) | YES  |     | NULL    |       |
| name  | text    | YES  |     | NULL    |       |
| color | text    | YES  |     | NULL    |       |
+-------+---------+------+-----+---------+-------+
3 rows in set (0.13 sec)

mysql> DROP TABLE IF EXISTS fruit ;
Query OK, 0 rows affected (0.19 sec)

mysql> SHOW TABLES ;
Empty set (0.00 sec)

mysql> _
```

The **EXPLAIN** query reveals the format of the "fruit" table which allows the "id" field to contain integers up to 11 digits long – in actuality this is limited to values between the range of -2147483648 to 2147483647.

In this example "YES" denotes that each field is allowed to contain no value, defined by the **NULL** keyword. Each field has, in fact, been created with no default value, so does contain a **NULL** value. Note that **NULL** represents absolutely no value – this is not the same as an empty string that is represented by "".

Hot tip

MySQL queries use a version of the Structured Query Language (SQL) in which each query must end with a semi-colon, but the **SOURCE** keyword simply describes a path that need not end with a semi-colon.

Don't forget

You can format the column definitions in an SQL file for better readability – additional spaces and line breaks are ignored.

Defining data types

The table below describes the range of data type specifiers that can be used to define database table columns. It is advisable to specify the permitted data type precisely. For instance, if a column only contains short strings use **VARCHAR()** rather than **TEXT**.

Type:	Value:
INT	An integer -2,147,483,648 to 2,147,483,647
DECIMAL	A floating point number that can specify the number of permissible digits. For example, DECIMAL(5,2) permits -999.99 to 999.99
DOUBLE	A long double-precision floating point number
DATE	A date in the YYYY-MM-DD format
TIME	A time in the HH:MM:SS format
DATETIME	A combined date and time in the format YYYY-MM-DD HH:MM:SS
YEAR	A year 1901-2155 in either YY or YYYY format
TIMESTAMP	Automatic date and time of last record entry
CHAR()	A string of defined fixed length up to 255 characters long. For example, CHAR(100) pads a smaller string to make it 100 characters long
VARCHAR()	A string of variable length up to 255 characters long that is stored without padding
TEXT	A string up to 65,535 characters long
BLOB	A binary type for variable data
ENUM	A single string value from a defined list. For example, ENUM("red", "green", "blue") allows entry of any one of these three colors only
SET	A string or multiple strings from a defined list. For example, SET("red", "green", "blue") allows entry of any one, or more, of these colors

The SQL script listed opposite creates a table that includes data type specifiers in the column definitions. The "id" column only accepts integer values. The date and time of each entry is automatically recorded in the "date" column. The "first_name" and "last_name" columns may each contain up to 20 characters.

1 Launch a plain text editor, such as Notepad, and create a query defining a table with columns of various data types
CREATE TABLE IF NOT EXISTS user_log

```
(
  id          INT ,
  date        TIMESTAMP ,
  first_name  VARCHAR(20) ,
  last_name   VARCHAR(20)
) ;
```

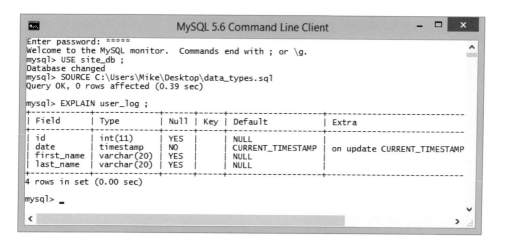

data_types.sql

2 Save the file on your desktop as **data_types.sql** then launch the MySQL Command Line Client and log in as a user with full access privileges, such as root

3 Next, issue a query to use the established database
USE site_db ;

4 Now, implement the SQL query by stating the source path to the SQL file on your system, such as
SOURCE C:\Users\Mike\Desktop\data_types.sql

5 Issue a query to confirm the table's existence and format
EXPLAIN user_log ;

```
MySQL 5.6 Command Line Client                      – □ ✕

Enter password: *****
Welcome to the MySQL monitor.  Commands end with ; or \g.
mysql> USE site_db ;
Database changed
mysql> SOURCE C:\Users\Mike\Desktop\data_types.sql
Query OK, 0 rows affected (0.39 sec)

mysql> EXPLAIN user_log ;
+------------+-------------+------+-----+-------------------+-----------------------------+
| Field      | Type        | Null | Key | Default           | Extra                       |
+------------+-------------+------+-----+-------------------+-----------------------------+
| id         | int(11)     | YES  |     | NULL              |                             |
| date       | timestamp   | NO   |     | CURRENT_TIMESTAMP | on update CURRENT_TIMESTAMP |
| first_name | varchar(20) | YES  |     | NULL              |                             |
| last_name  | varchar(20) | YES  |     | NULL              |                             |
+------------+-------------+------+-----+-------------------+-----------------------------+
4 rows in set (0.00 sec)

mysql>
```

Adding modifiers

In addition to specifying permissible data types, with the keywords on the previous page, the modifier keywords in the following table can optionally be used to further control column content:

Modifier:	Purpose:
NOT NULL	Insists that each record must include a data value in this column
UNIQUE	Insists that records may not duplicate any entry in this column
AUTO_INCREMENT	Available only for numeric columns, to automatically generate a number that is one more than the previous value in that column
DEFAULT	Specifies a value to be used where no value is stated for this column when a record is inserted
PRIMARY KEY	Specifies the column, or columns, to be used as the primary key for that table

Hot tip

The **PRIMARY KEY** modifier is described in more detail on page 92.

When it is essential that a record must include a value for a column, that column should be defined with the **NOT NULL** modifier. This allows an empty string "" to be stored there but does not allow that column to be empty or **NULL**. When the data stored in a column should never be duplicated that column should be defined with the **UNIQUE** modifier. For instance, to avoid the accidental duplication of product codes. The **AUTO_INCREMENT** modifier is particularly useful to automatically generate incremental identity numbers for each row – the first row will be numbered 1, the second row 2, and so on. Setting a column **DEFAULT** allows records to be inserted without tediously requiring a value for a column that is usually constant. For instance, a "quantity" column might usually contain a value of 1 in each record – so 1 could be set as its default value.

The SQL script listed opposite creates a table that uses modifiers in its column definitions to control the permissible content. The "id" column automatically numbers each row and the "quantity" column will contain 1 unless another value is inserted. All the other columns must contain values – they can't be empty or **NULL**.

1 Launch a plain text editor, such as Notepad, and create a query defining a table with columns of various modifiers

```
CREATE TABLE IF NOT EXISTS products
(
   id          INT UNIQUE    AUTO_INCREMENT ,
   code        INT           NOT NULL ,
   name        VARCHAR(25)   NOT NULL ,
   quantity    INT           DEFAULT 1 NULL ,
   price       DECIMAL(6,2)  NOT NULL
) ;
```

modifiers.sql

2 Save the file on your desktop as **modifiers.sql** then launch the MySQL Command Line Client and log in as a user with full access privileges, such as root

3 Next, issue a query to use the established database

USE site_db ;

4 Now, implement the SQL query by stating the source path to the SQL file on your system, such as

SOURCE C:\Users\Mike\Desktop\modifiers.sql

5 Issue a query to confirm the table's existence and format

EXPLAIN products ;

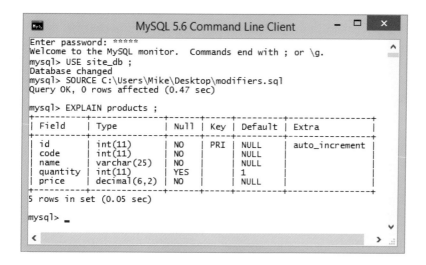

```
┌──┐              MySQL 5.6 Command Line Client        ─ □ ✕
│My│
Enter password: *****
Welcome to the MySQL monitor.  Commands end with ; or \g.
mysql> USE site_db ;
Database changed
mysql> SOURCE C:\Users\Mike\Desktop\modifiers.sql
Query OK, 0 rows affected (0.47 sec)

mysql> EXPLAIN products ;
+----------+--------------+------+-----+---------+----------------+
| Field    | Type         | Null | Key | Default | Extra          |
+----------+--------------+------+-----+---------+----------------+
| id       | int(11)      | NO   | PRI | NULL    | auto_increment |
| code     | int(11)      | NO   |     | NULL    |                |
| name     | varchar(25)  | NO   |     | NULL    |                |
| quantity | int(11)      | YES  |     | 1       |                |
| price    | decimal(6,2) | NO   |     | NULL    |                |
+----------+--------------+------+-----+---------+----------------+
5 rows in set (0.05 sec)

mysql> _
```

Hot tip

The right-hand column in this illustration is headed "Extra" and notes the "auto_increment" modifier.

Setting primary keys

A **PRIMARY KEY** is a "constraint" that is applied to a column to uniquely identify each row of that database table. It ensures that the values in each row of that column are unique and never change, so those values can be used to reference any specific row.

By setting the **PRIMARY KEY** constraint it is possible to manipulate data on specific rows of the database table.

Any column can be set as the **PRIMARY KEY** but it is often the first column that is used to provide a unique identifying number.

Any column set as the **PRIMARY KEY** must meet these criteria:

- Each field in that column must have a value – it may not be empty or have a **NULL** value

- Each value in that column must be unique – there must be no duplications

- Each value in that column can never be modified or updated

- Each value in that column cannot be re-used – when a row is deleted its **PRIMARY KEY** value cannot be re-assigned as the **PRIMARY KEY** value of a new row

Don't forget

A table's **PRIMARY KEY** must be a unique constant value.

Notice in the previous example that MySQL automatically sets the "id" column as the **PRIMARY KEY** because of the **UNIQUE** modifier that was included in that column's definition. This is indicated in the output from the **EXPLAIN** query, on page 91, by the term "PRI" listed under the "Key" heading. This is logical because any column that may only contain unique values can be used to identify each table row by that column's value.

The **PRIMARY KEY** constraint can be set by adding the **PRIMARY KEY** keywords to the column definition in the **CREATE TABLE** query. Alternatively, a **PRIMARY KEY** can be set elsewhere in the **CREATE TABLE** query by stating the name of the column in parentheses after the **PRIMARY KEY** keywords.

The SQL script on the opposite page creates two tables with a **PRIMARY KEY** column set by different methods. Each table can reference any specific row by its "id" value. Notice that the **EXPLAIN** queries confirm both **PRIMARY KEY** settings.

1 Launch a plain text editor, such as Notepad, and create a query defining two tables with specified primary keys

```
CREATE TABLE IF NOT EXISTS cups
(
  id           INT AUTO_INCREMENT   PRIMARY KEY ,
  cup_pattern  VARCHAR(25)
) ;

CREATE TABLE IF NOT EXISTS pots
(
  id           INT     AUTO_INCREMENT ,
  pot_pattern  VARCHAR(25) , PRIMARY KEY( id )
) ;
```

primary_key.sql

2 Save the file on your desktop as **primary_key.sql** then log in to the MySQL Command Line Client as root and issue a query to use the established database
USE site_db ;

3 Now, implement the SQL query by stating the source path to the SQL file on your system, such as
SOURCE C:\Users\Mike\Desktop\primary_key.sql

4 Issue a query to confirm the tables' existence and format
EXPLAIN cups ; EXPLAIN pots ;

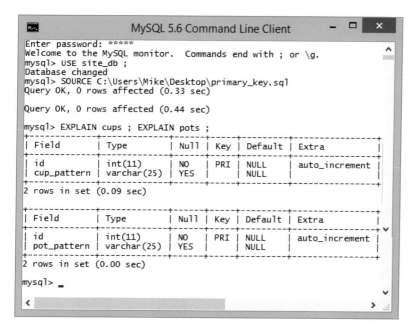

```
                    MySQL 5.6 Command Line Client         _  □  ×
Enter password: *****
Welcome to the MySQL monitor.  Commands end with ; or \g.
mysql> USE site_db ;
Database changed
mysql> SOURCE C:\Users\Mike\Desktop\primary_key.sql
Query OK, 0 rows affected (0.33 sec)

Query OK, 0 rows affected (0.44 sec)

mysql> EXPLAIN cups ; EXPLAIN pots ;
+-------------+-------------+------+-----+---------+----------------+
| Field       | Type        | Null | Key | Default | Extra          |
+-------------+-------------+------+-----+---------+----------------+
| id          | int(11)     | NO   | PRI | NULL    | auto_increment |
| cup_pattern | varchar(25) | YES  |     | NULL    |                |
+-------------+-------------+------+-----+---------+----------------+
2 rows in set (0.09 sec)

+-------------+-------------+------+-----+---------+----------------+
| Field       | Type        | Null | Key | Default | Extra          |
+-------------+-------------+------+-----+---------+----------------+
| id          | int(11)     | NO   | PRI | NULL    | auto_increment |
| pot_pattern | varchar(25) | YES  |     | NULL    |                |
+-------------+-------------+------+-----+---------+----------------+
2 rows in set (0.00 sec)

mysql>
```

Altering tables

The format of an existing database table can be changed with an **ALTER TABLE** query. This query can make a single alteration or specify a number of alterations as a comma-separated list.

An **ALTER TABLE** query can **ADD** a complete new **COLUMN** to an existing table, like this:

```
ALTER TABLE table-name ;
ADD COLUMN column-name data-type optional-modifier/s ;
```

It can also **ADD** a **PRIMARY KEY** to an existing column definition using this syntax:

```
ALTER TABLE table-name ;
ADD PRIMARY KEY ( column-name ) ;
```

Hot tip

In the **ADD COLUMN** and **DROP COLUMN** examples the **COLUMN** keyword is optional – it is what the manual calls "a pure noise word" that is only there to aid readability.

An **ALTER TABLE** query can **CHANGE** the name of an existing column. The new column will not inherit any data type or modifiers specified to the original column – these must be set anew in the **ALTER TABLE** query, like this:

```
ALTER TABLE table-name ;
CHANGE old-column-name new-column-name
                data-type optional-modifier/s ;
```

An **ALTER TABLE** query can also permanently delete an entire column from the table using the **DROP COLUMN** keywords:

```
ALTER TABLE table-name ;
DROP COLUMN column-name ;
```

The following SQL script demonstrates all these possibilities:

alter_table.sql

1. Launch a plain text editor, such as Notepad, and create a query defining a table with three columns
```
CREATE TABLE IF NOT EXISTS pans
(
  id            INT           NOT NULL ,
  pattern       VARCHAR(25)   NOT NULL ,
  price         DECIMAL( 6,2 )
) ;
```

2. Next, add a query to confirm the table's format
```
EXPLAIN pans ;
```

3 Now, add a query to update the table
ALTER TABLE pans
ADD PRIMARY KEY (id) ,
ADD COLUMN code INT UNIQUE NOT NULL ,
CHANGE pattern pan_pattern VARCHAR(25) NOT NULL ,
DROP COLUMN price ;

4 Finally, add a query to confirm the altered table format
EXPLAIN pans ;

5 Save the file on your desktop as **alter_table.sql** then log in to the MySQL Command Line Client as root and issue a query to use the established database
USE site_db ;

6 Implement the SQL query by stating the source path to the SQL file on your system, such as
SOURCE C:\Users\Mike\Desktop\alter_table.sql

Beware

Care should be taken in using **DROP COLUMN** as it will remove any data that is contained in that column – the data cannot be recovered.

```
MySQL 5.6 Command Line Client

Enter password: *****
Welcome to the MySQL monitor.  Commands end with ; or \g.
mysql> USE site_db ;
Database changed
mysql> SOURCE C:\Users\Mike\Desktop\alter_table.sql
Query OK, 0 rows affected (0.50 sec)

+---------+-------------+------+-----+---------+-------+
| Field   | Type        | Null | Key | Default | Extra |
+---------+-------------+------+-----+---------+-------+
| id      | int(11)     | NO   |     | NULL    |       |
| pattern | varchar(25) | NO   |     | NULL    |       |
| price   | decimal(6,2)| YES  |     | NULL    |       |
+---------+-------------+------+-----+---------+-------+
3 rows in set (0.00 sec)

Query OK, 0 rows affected (0.94 sec)
Records: 0  Duplicates: 0  Warnings: 0

+-------------+-------------+------+-----+---------+-------+
| Field       | Type        | Null | Key | Default | Extra |
+-------------+-------------+------+-----+---------+-------+
| id          | int(11)     | NO   | PRI | NULL    |       |
| pan_pattern | varchar(25) | NO   |     | NULL    |       |
| code        | int(11)     | NO   | UNI | NULL    |       |
+-------------+-------------+------+-----+---------+-------+
3 rows in set (0.02 sec)

mysql> _
```

Don't forget

Well designed database tables should never need to be altered if they anticipate all likely future requirements.

Summary

- The **USE DATABASE** query selects a database to work with

- The names of all the tables in a database can be revealed with the **SHOW TABLES** query

- The format of a table can be examined with an **EXPLAIN** query

- A new table can be created with the **CREATE TABLE** query

- The **CREATE TABLE** query can be qualified with **IF NOT EXISTS** to ensure that a table of the specified name does not already exist

- An existing table can be deleted with a **DROP TABLE** query

- The **DROP TABLE** query can be qualified with **IF EXISTS** to ensure that a table of the specified name already exists

- A column definition should specify the data type that it may contain using recognized data type keywords such as **INT, DOUBLE, DECIMAL, DATETIME, TIMESTAMP, DATE, TIME, YEAR, CHAR(), VARCHAR(), TEXT, BLOB, ENUM** or **SET**

- Optionally, a column definition may specify a field modifier to further control that column's permissible content to make it **NOT NULL, AUTO_INCREMENT, UNIQUE, DEFAULT** or **PRIMARY KEY**

- When a column is set as a **PRIMARY KEY** each row must contain unique unalterable data in that column which can be used to identify each row of that table

- An **ALTER TABLE** query can be used to **ADD** a new column to an existing table

- An **ALTER TABLE** query can be used to **CHANGE** a column in an existing table

- An **ALTER TABLE** query can be used to delete a column from an existing table with the **DROP** keyword

6 Handling data

This chapter demonstrates how to make SQL statements to store and retrieve data with MySQL database tables.

Inserting data

Data can be inserted into an existing database table with an **INSERT INTO** query that first specifies the table name. The SQL **VALUES** keyword then specifies the actual data to be inserted as a comma-separated list within parentheses, like this:

INSERT INTO *table-name* VALUES (*value* , *value*) ;

Each **INSERT INTO** query inserts just one row into the database table. A data value must be specified for each column – and in the corresponding order. The data to be inserted must also match the data type in each column's definition or an error will be generated. The **NULL** keyword can be specified to leave a field empty if that column's definition allows **NULL** values.

The **INSERT INTO** query can be improved by adding a "columns list" to explicitly specify the table column into which each value should be inserted. This changes the syntax of the **INSERT INTO** query to look like this:

INSERT INTO *table-name* (*column-name* , *column-name*)
VALUES (*value* , *value*) , (*value* , *value*) , (*value* , *value*) ;

When the **INSERT INTO** query contains a columns list the MySQL Server matches each value to the specified column in the order in which they are listed – the value listed first will be matched to the column listed first, the value listed second will be matched to the column listed second, and so on. The number of listed values must match the number of listed columns, but the columns need not be listed in the order in which they appear in the database table. Additionally, a columns list need not list all the columns in the table providing that omitted columns allow **NULL** values. This allows an **INSERT INTO** query to insert only partial rows.

It is strongly recommended that all **INSERT INTO** queries should include a columns list so that the query may remain valid in the event that the table gets altered.

All data contained in a table can be displayed with a **SELECT** query using the * wildcard and the **FROM** keyword like this:

SELECT * FROM *table-name* ;

The SQL script opposite creates a table then inserts some data into its columns before selecting the entire content for display.

Beware

Any text values to be inserted into a database must be enclosed within quotation marks.

1 Launch a plain text editor, such as Notepad, and create a query defining a table with three columns
CREATE TABLE IF NOT EXISTS prints
(
 id **INT AUTO_INCREMENT PRIMARY KEY** ,
 name **VARCHAR(32)** ,
 price **DECIMAL(6,2)**
) ;

insert_data.sql

2 Next, add a query to insert three records into this table
INSERT INTO prints (name , price)
VALUES (**"Merry Structure"** , **29.99**) ,
 (**"Heavy Red"** , **24.99**) , (**"Black Lines"** , **45.99**) ;

3 Now, add a query to display all records from this table
SELECT * FROM prints ;

4 Save the file on your desktop as **insert_data.sql** then launch the MySQL Command Line Client and issue a query to use the established database
USE site_db ;

5 Now, implement the SQL query by stating the source path to the SQL file on your system, such as
SOURCE C:\Users\Mike\Desktop\insert_data.sql

Don't forget

Always include a columns list when inserting data into a table to explicitly specify where the data should be placed.

66

Updating columns

All the data contained within a column of a database table can be changed with an **UPDATE** query, that has this syntax:

UPDATE *table-name* **SET** *column-name = value* ;

The **UPDATE** keyword is followed by the name of the table to work with and the **SET** keyword specifies the name of the column to be updated with a new specified value.

Note that this SQL query will update every field in the specified column with the single specified value.

update_all.sql

1. Launch a plain text editor, such as Notepad, and create a query defining a table with four columns
```
CREATE TABLE IF NOT EXISTS towels
(
  id            INT AUTO_INCREMENT PRIMARY KEY ,
  name          CHAR(16) ,
  color         CHAR(16) ,
  price         DECIMAL(6,2)
) ;
```

2. Next, add a query to insert five records into this table
```
INSERT INTO towels ( name , color , price )
VALUES  ( "Dolphin" , "Blue" , 9.99 ) ,
( "Wine" , "Maroon" , 12.99 ) ,
( "Harvest" , "Beige" , 7.99 ) ,
( "Daisy" , "Lilac" , 8.99 ) ,
( "Starburst" , "Yellow" , 10.99 ) ;
```

3. Now, add a query to display all records from this table
```
SELECT * FROM towels ;
```

4. Add queries to update the "color" column of this table and display all records to see the updated version
```
UPDATE towels SET color = "White" ;
SELECT * FROM towels ;
```

5. Add queries to update the "price" column of this table and display all records to see the updated version again
```
UPDATE towels SET price = 5.99 ;
SELECT * FROM towels ;
```

6 Save the file on your desktop as **update_all.sql** then launch the MySQL Command Line Client and issue a query to use the established database
USE site_db ;

7 Now, implement the SQL queries by stating the source path to the SQL file on your system, such as
SOURCE C:\Users\Mike\Desktop\update_all.sql

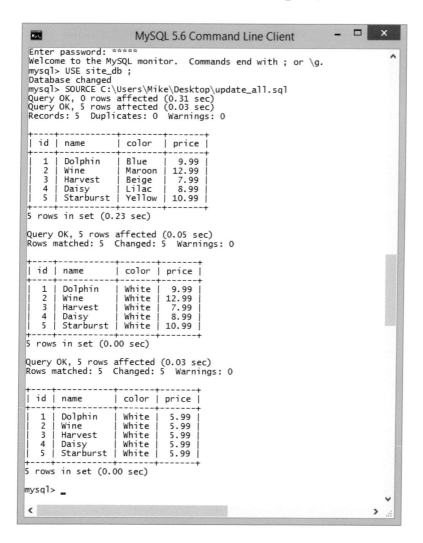

```
MySQL 5.6 Command Line Client                    _  □  ×

Enter password: *****
Welcome to the MySQL monitor.  Commands end with ; or \g.
mysql> USE site_db ;
Database changed
mysql> SOURCE C:\Users\Mike\Desktop\update_all.sql
Query OK, 0 rows affected (0.31 sec)
Query OK, 5 rows affected (0.03 sec)
Records: 5  Duplicates: 0  Warnings: 0

+----+-----------+--------+-------+
| id | name      | color  | price |
+----+-----------+--------+-------+
|  1 | Dolphin   | Blue   |  9.99 |
|  2 | Wine      | Maroon | 12.99 |
|  3 | Harvest   | Beige  |  7.99 |
|  4 | Daisy     | Lilac  |  8.99 |
|  5 | Starburst | Yellow | 10.99 |
+----+-----------+--------+-------+
5 rows in set (0.23 sec)

Query OK, 5 rows affected (0.05 sec)
Rows matched: 5  Changed: 5  Warnings: 0

+----+-----------+--------+-------+
| id | name      | color  | price |
+----+-----------+--------+-------+
|  1 | Dolphin   | White  |  9.99 |
|  2 | Wine      | White  | 12.99 |
|  3 | Harvest   | White  |  7.99 |
|  4 | Daisy     | White  |  8.99 |
|  5 | Starburst | White  | 10.99 |
+----+-----------+--------+-------+
5 rows in set (0.00 sec)

Query OK, 5 rows affected (0.03 sec)
Rows matched: 5  Changed: 5  Warnings: 0

+----+-----------+--------+-------+
| id | name      | color  | price |
+----+-----------+--------+-------+
|  1 | Dolphin   | White  |  5.99 |
|  2 | Wine      | White  |  5.99 |
|  3 | Harvest   | White  |  5.99 |
|  4 | Daisy     | White  |  5.99 |
|  5 | Starburst | White  |  5.99 |
+----+-----------+--------+-------+
5 rows in set (0.00 sec)

mysql> _
```

Hot tip

It is sometimes useful to remove all values in a column using an **UPDATE** query to set each field to **NULL** – providing the column definition allows **NULL** values.

Updating fields

Usually an **UPDATE** query will be required to change data contained in a particular field of a column on a specific row. The row can be identified by adding the **WHERE** keyword to the **UPDATE** query to match a value in a specified column. The syntax of the specific **UPDATE** query now looks like this:

UPDATE *table-name*
SET *column-name* = *value* WHERE *column-name* = *value* ;

A single **UPDATE** query can also change multiple column values on a specific row by making multiple *column-name* = *value* statements as a comma-delimited list after the **SET** keyword.

If the **WHERE** keyword identifies multiple rows that each have the same specified value they will each get updated with the new value – possibly causing accidental data loss. It is therefore safer to identify the row by its **PRIMARY KEY** value as this is guaranteed to be unique so multiple rows cannot be accidentally updated.

update_where.sql

Beware

If the **WHERE** keyword is omitted from an **UPDATE** query all rows will be updated – lost data cannot be recovered.

1. Launch a plain text editor, such as Notepad, and create a query defining a table with four columns
```
CREATE TABLE IF NOT EXISTS tiles
(
  id          INT AUTO_INCREMENT PRIMARY KEY ,
  pattern     CHAR(16) ,
  color       CHAR(16) ,
  price       DECIMAL(6,2)
) ;
```

2. Next, add a query to insert four records into this table
```
INSERT INTO tiles ( pattern , color , price )
VALUES ( "Spring" , "Green" , 9.99 ) ,
( "Summer" , "Yellow" , 12.99 ) ,
( "Autumn" , "Brown" , 9.99 ) ,
( "Winter" , "Blue" , 8.99 ) ;
```

3. Now, add a query to display all records from this table
```
SELECT * FROM tiles ;
```

4. Add a query to update the "pattern" column of this table by identifying its current value
```
UPDATE tiles
SET pattern = "Fall" WHERE pattern = "Autumn" ;
```

5 Add queries to update other columns by identifying the current "color", "price", and "id" values and display them
UPDATE tiles SET color = **"Gold"** WHERE color = **"Yellow"** ;
UPDATE tiles SET price = **10.99** WHERE price = **9.99** ;
UPDATE tiles SET price = **11.99** WHERE id = **4** ;
SELECT * FROM tiles ;

6 Save the file on your desktop as **update_where.sql** then launch the MySQL Command Line Client and issue a query to use the established database
USE site_db ;

7 Now, implement the SQL queries by stating the source path to the SQL file on your system, such as
SOURCE C:\Users\Mike\Desktop\update_where.sql

Hot tip

Always attempt to **UPDATE** tables by identifying the row by its **PRIMARY KEY** value.

Deleting data

Rows can be removed from a database table with a **DELETE FROM** query. All rows can be removed with this syntax:

DELETE FROM *table-name* ;

More usually, a specific row can be removed from a table by adding the **WHERE** keyword to a **DELETE FROM** query to identify the row. The syntax of the **DELETE FROM** query now looks like this:

DELETE FROM *table-name* **WHERE** *column-name = value* ;

If the **WHERE** keyword identifies multiple rows that each have the same specified value they will each get deleted – possibly causing accidental data loss. It is therefore safer to identify the row by its **PRIMARY KEY** value as this is guaranteed to be unique so multiple rows cannot be accidentally deleted.

delete_from.sql

 1
Launch a plain text editor, such as Notepad, and create a query defining a table with four columns
```
CREATE TABLE IF NOT EXISTS pens
(
  id          INT AUTO_INCREMENT PRIMARY KEY ,
  maker       CHAR(32) ,
  model       CHAR(32) ,
  price       DECIMAL(6,2)
) ;
```

Don't forget

The **DELETE** keyword cannot be used to remove a table – you must use the **DROP** keyword for removal.

2
Next, add a query to insert four records into this table
```
INSERT INTO pens ( maker , model , price )
VALUES  ( "Montegrappa" , "Silver Dragon" , 950.00 ) ,
( "Paul Rossi" , "Egyptian Lady" , 650.00 ) ,
( "Michel Perchin" , "Red Cross" , 450.00 ) ,
( "Bexley" , "Poseidon Magnum" , 350.00 ) ;
```

3
Now, add a query to display all records from this table
```
SELECT * FROM pens ;
```

4
Add queries to individually delete rows by various column values then display the remaining records
```
DELETE FROM pens WHERE maker = "Montegrappa" ;
SELECT * FROM pens ;
DELETE FROM pens WHERE model = "Egyptian Lady" ;
SELECT * FROM pens ;
DELETE FROM pens WHERE price = 450.00 ;
SELECT * FROM pens ;
DELETE FROM pens WHERE id = 4 ; SELECT * FROM pens ;
```

...cont'd

5 Save the file on your desktop as **delete_from.sql** then launch the MySQL Command Line Client and issue a query to use the established database
USE site_db ;

6 Now, implement the SQL queries by stating the source path to the SQL file on your system, such as
SOURCE C:\Users\Mike\Desktop\delete_from.sql

Beware

If the **WHERE** keyword is omitted from a **DELETE FROM** query all rows will be deleted – lost data cannot be recovered.

Selecting data

The SQL query to view all data in a database table was introduced at the start of this chapter. The wildcard * character, meaning "all", can be replaced with a column name to retrieve only data from that particular column. The syntax of this query looks like this:

SELECT *column-name* **FROM** *table-name* ;

The following script creates and displays an entire table then selects individual columns for display.

selection.sql

1 Launch a plain text editor, such as Notepad, and create a query defining a table with four columns
```
CREATE TABLE IF NOT EXISTS paintings
(
  id            INT AUTO_INCREMENT PRIMARY KEY ,
  artists       CHAR(32) ,
  titles        CHAR(64) ,
  styles        CHAR(16)
) ;
```

2 Next, add a query to insert four records into this table
```
INSERT INTO paintings ( artists , titles , styles )
VALUES
( "Salvador Dali" , "Meditative Rose" , "Surrealist" ) ,
( "Henri Matisse" , "Blue Hair" , "Impressionist" ) ,
( "Pablo Picasso" , "Girl Reading" , "Cubist" ) ,
( "Marc Chegall" , "Bonjour Paris" , "Primitivist" ) ;
```

3 Now, add a query to display all records from this table
```
SELECT * FROM paintings ;
```

4 Add a query to individually display the "artists" column
```
SELECT artists FROM paintings ;
```

5 Add a query to individually display the "titles" column
```
SELECT titles FROM paintings ;
```

6 Add a query to individually display the "styles" column
```
SELECT styles FROM paintings ;
```

7 Save the file on your desktop as **selection.sql** then launch the MySQL Command Line Client and issue a query to use the established database
USE site_db ;

8 Now, implement the SQL queries by stating the source path to the SQL file on your system, such as
SOURCE C:\Users\Mike\Desktop\selection.sql

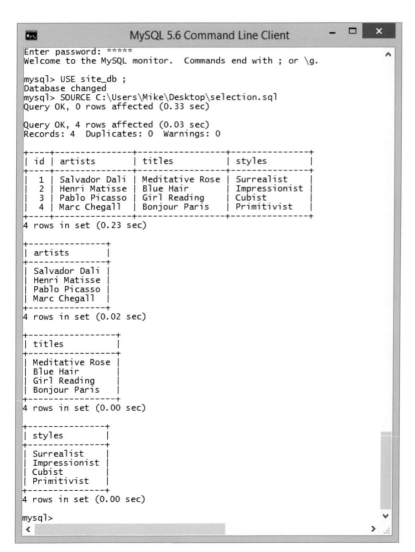

```
                    MySQL 5.6 Command Line Client        _  □  ×
Enter password: *****
Welcome to the MySQL monitor.  Commands end with ; or \g.

mysql> USE site_db ;
Database changed
mysql> SOURCE C:\Users\Mike\Desktop\selection.sql
Query OK, 0 rows affected (0.33 sec)

Query OK, 4 rows affected (0.03 sec)
Records: 4  Duplicates: 0  Warnings: 0

+----+---------------+----------------+---------------+
| id | artists       | titles         | styles        |
+----+---------------+----------------+---------------+
|  1 | Salvador Dali | Meditative Rose | Surrealist   |
|  2 | Henri Matisse | Blue Hair      | Impressionist |
|  3 | Pablo Picasso | Girl Reading   | Cubist        |
|  4 | Marc Chegall  | Bonjour Paris  | Primitivist   |
+----+---------------+----------------+---------------+
4 rows in set (0.23 sec)

+---------------+
| artists       |
+---------------+
| Salvador Dali |
| Henri Matisse |
| Pablo Picasso |
| Marc Chegall  |
+---------------+
4 rows in set (0.02 sec)

+----------------+
| titles         |
+----------------+
| Meditative Rose |
| Blue Hair      |
| Girl Reading   |
| Bonjour Paris  |
+----------------+
4 rows in set (0.00 sec)

+---------------+
| styles        |
+---------------+
| Surrealist    |
| Impressionist |
| Cubist        |
| Primitivist   |
+---------------+
4 rows in set (0.00 sec)

mysql>
```

Don't forget

Notice that the data is retrieved in the same "top-down" order as it is stored in each column.

Retrieving columns

A **SELECT** query can return the data from multiple columns by including the required column names as a comma-separated list in the query. The syntax to get multiple column data looks like this:

SELECT *column-name* , *column-name* **FROM** *table-name* ;

The following script creates and displays an entire table then selects multiple columns for display.

select_columns.sql

1. Launch a plain text editor, such as Notepad, and create a query defining a table with four columns
```
CREATE TABLE IF NOT EXISTS phones
(
  id          INT AUTO_INCREMENT PRIMARY KEY ,
  make        CHAR(16) ,
  model       CHAR(16) ,
  platform    CHAR(16)
) ;
```

2. Next, add a query to insert four records into this table
```
INSERT INTO phones ( make , model , platform )
VALUES
( "Apple" , "iPhone" , "iOS" ) ,
( "RIM" , "Curve" , "BlackBerry" ) ,
( "HTC" , "Desire" , "Android" ) ,
( "Nokia" , "Lumia" , "Windows" ) ;
```

3. Now, add a query to display all records from this table
```
SELECT * FROM phones ;
```

4. Add a query to display the "id" and "make" columns
```
SELECT id , make FROM phones ;
```

5. Add a query to display the "make" and "model" columns
```
SELECT make , model FROM phones ;
```

6. Add a query to display the "id" and "platform" columns
```
SELECT id , platform FROM phones ;
```

7 Save the file on your desktop as **select_columns.sql** then launch the MySQL Command Line Client and issue a query to use the established database
USE site_db ;

8 Now, implement the SQL queries by stating the source path to the SQL file on your system, such as
SOURCE C:\Users\Mike\Desktop\select_columns.sql

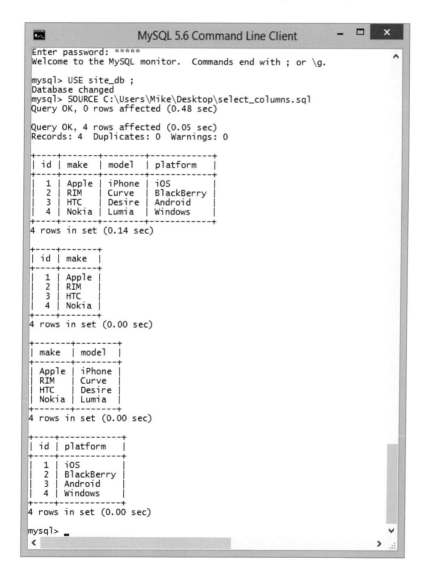

```
MySQL 5.6 Command Line Client                    –  □  ×

Enter password: *****
Welcome to the MySQL monitor.  Commands end with ; or \g.

mysql> USE site_db ;
Database changed
mysql> SOURCE C:\Users\Mike\Desktop\select_columns.sql
Query OK, 0 rows affected (0.48 sec)

Query OK, 4 rows affected (0.05 sec)
Records: 4  Duplicates: 0  Warnings: 0

+----+-------+--------+------------+
| id | make  | model  | platform   |
+----+-------+--------+------------+
|  1 | Apple | iPhone | iOS        |
|  2 | RIM   | Curve  | BlackBerry |
|  3 | HTC   | Desire | Android    |
|  4 | Nokia | Lumia  | Windows    |
+----+-------+--------+------------+
4 rows in set (0.14 sec)

+----+-------+
| id | make  |
+----+-------+
|  1 | Apple |
|  2 | RIM   |
|  3 | HTC   |
|  4 | Nokia |
+----+-------+
4 rows in set (0.00 sec)

+-------+--------+
| make  | model  |
+-------+--------+
| Apple | iPhone |
| RIM   | Curve  |
| HTC   | Desire |
| Nokia | Lumia  |
+-------+--------+
4 rows in set (0.00 sec)

+----+------------+
| id | platform   |
+----+------------+
|  1 | iOS        |
|  2 | BlackBerry |
|  3 | Android    |
|  4 | Windows    |
+----+------------+
4 rows in set (0.00 sec)

mysql> _
```

Don't forget

SELECT queries only retrieve a copy of data contained in the specified table – the table is unaltered.

Retrieving rows

A **SELECT** query can retrieve a specific row from a database table if it includes the **WHERE** keyword to identify the required row. The row should be identified by its **PRIMARY KEY** value to prevent possible duplication. The syntax of a **SELECT** query to retrieve a specific row looks like this:

```
SELECT * FROM table-name WHERE column-name = value ;
```

Additionally, a **WHERE** clause in a **SELECT** query can specify a list of alternative values for comparison with column data using the **IN** keyword. This is followed by a comma-separated list of values within a single pair of parentheses. So the syntax looks like this:

```
SELECT * FROM table-name
WHERE column-name IN ( value , value , value ) ;
```

When the column data matches any one of the values in the list, the **WHERE** clause evaluates as **TRUE** and data is returned for that row. The comparison can be inverted by preceding the **IN** keyword with the **NOT** keyword. Then the **WHERE** clause only evaluates as **TRUE** when no list value matches the column data.

select_rows.sql

1 Launch a plain text editor, such as Notepad, and create a query defining a table with four columns
```
CREATE TABLE IF NOT EXISTS coffee_machines
(
  id            INT AUTO_INCREMENT PRIMARY KEY ,
  make          CHAR(16) ,
  model         CHAR(16) ,
  price         DECIMAL(6,2)
) ;
```

2 Next, add a query to insert five records into this table
```
INSERT INTO coffee_machines ( make , model , price )
VALUES
( "Krups" , "Dolce Gusto" , 140.00 ) ,
( "Gaggia" , "Cubika" , 170.00 ) ,
( "DeLonghi" , "Magnifica" , 500.00 ) ,
( "Magimix" , "Nespresso" , 300.00 ) ,
( "Cuisinart" , "Espresso" , 280.00 ) ;
```

3 Now, add a query to display one row from this table
```
SELECT * FROM coffee_machines WHERE id = 3 ;
```

4 Add a query to display two particular rows
SELECT * FROM coffee_machines
WHERE make **IN** (**"Krups"** , **"Gaggia"**) ;

5 Finally, add a query to display all other rows
SELECT * FROM coffee_machines
WHERE make **NOT IN** (**"Krups"** , **"Gaggia"**) ;

6 Save the file on your desktop as **select_rows.sql** then
launch the MySQL Command Line Client and issue a
query to use the established database
USE site_db ;

7 Now, implement the SQL queries by stating the source
path to the SQL file on your system, such as
SOURCE C:\Users\Mike\Desktop\select_rows.sql

```
Enter password: *****
Welcome to the MySQL monitor.  Commands end with ; or \g.

mysql> USE site_db ;
Database changed
mysql> SOURCE C:\Users\Mike\Desktop\select_rows.sql
Query OK, 0 rows affected (0.28 sec)

Query OK, 5 rows affected (0.03 sec)
Records: 5  Duplicates: 0  Warnings: 0

+----+----------+----------+--------+
| id | make     | model    | price  |
+----+----------+----------+--------+
|  3 | DeLonghi | Magnifica | 500.00 |
+----+----------+----------+--------+
1 row in set (0.14 sec)

+----+--------+-------------+--------+
| id | make   | model       | price  |
+----+--------+-------------+--------+
|  1 | Krups  | Dolce Gusto | 140.00 |
|  2 | Gaggia | Cubika      | 170.00 |
+----+--------+-------------+--------+
2 rows in set (0.00 sec)

+----+----------+----------+--------+
| id | make     | model    | price  |
+----+----------+----------+--------+
|  3 | DeLonghi | Magnifica | 500.00 |
|  4 | Magimix  | Nespresso | 300.00 |
|  5 | Cuisinart | Espresso | 280.00 |
+----+----------+----------+--------+
3 rows in set (0.00 sec)

mysql>
```

MySQL 5.6 Command Line Client

Hot tip

SQL queries comprise
one, or more "clauses".
Each clause consists of
a keyword and data. For
instance, **WHERE id = 3**
is known as a **WHERE**
clause.

Sorting data

The data returned by a **SELECT** query can be explicitly sorted into a specified order using an **ORDER BY** clause, with this syntax:

SELECT *column-name* **FROM** *table-name* **ORDER BY** *column-name* ;

When the **ORDER BY** keywords are followed by a table column name the retrieved data will be sorted into order based upon the type of data in the specified column. Typically, if the column data type is numerical, the retrieved data will be sorted in ascending numerical order. If the column data type is textual the retrieved data will be sorted into alphabetical order from A through Z.

The SQL example script listed below demonstrates both numerical and alphabetical sorting of retrieved data.

order_by.sql

1. Launch a plain text editor, such as Notepad, and create a query defining a table with four columns
```
CREATE TABLE IF NOT EXISTS watches
(
  id        INT AUTO_INCREMENT PRIMARY KEY ,
  model     CHAR(16) ,
  style     CHAR(16) ,
  price     DECIMAL(6,2)
) ;
```

2. Next, add a query to insert five records into this table
```
INSERT INTO watches ( model , style , price )
VALUES
( "Boston" , "Gents" , 70.00 ) ,
( "Avante" , "Ladies" , 90.00 ) ,
( "Club" , "Gents" , 60.00 ) ,
( "Denver" , "Ladies" , 80.00 ) ,
( "Eton" , "Gents" , 50.00 ) ;
```

3. Now, add a query to display all columns of all records in this table sorted by ascending "price" order
```
SELECT * FROM watches ORDER BY price ;
```

4. Add a query to display all models and prices in this table sorted by alphabetical "model" order
```
SELECT model , price FROM watches ORDER BY model ;
```

5 Finally, add a query to display all models and styles in this table sorted by alphabetical "style" order
SELECT model , style **FROM** watches **ORDER BY** style ;

6 Save the file on your desktop as **order_by.sql** then launch the MySQL Command Line Client and issue a query to use the established database
USE site_db ;

7 Now, implement the SQL queries by stating the source path to the SQL file on your system, such as
SOURCE C:\Users\Mike\Desktop\order_by.sql

Beware

An **ORDER BY** clause must only appear as the final clause of a **SELECT** query – otherwise an error is generated.

```
MySQL 5.6 Command Line Client

Enter password: *****
Welcome to the MySQL monitor.  Commands end with ; or \g.

mysql> USE site_db ;
Database changed
mysql> SOURCE C:\Users\Mike\Desktop\order_by.sql
Query OK, 0 rows affected (0.50 sec)

Query OK, 5 rows affected (0.08 sec)
Records: 5  Duplicates: 0  Warnings: 0

+----+--------+--------+-------+
| id | model  | style  | price |
+----+--------+--------+-------+
|  5 | Eton   | Gents  | 50.00 |
|  3 | Club   | Gents  | 60.00 |
|  1 | Boston | Gents  | 70.00 |
|  4 | Denver | Ladies | 80.00 |
|  2 | Avante | Ladies | 90.00 |
+----+--------+--------+-------+
5 rows in set (0.16 sec)

+--------+-------+
| model  | price |
+--------+-------+
| Avante | 90.00 |
| Boston | 70.00 |
| Club   | 60.00 |
| Denver | 80.00 |
| Eton   | 50.00 |
+--------+-------+
5 rows in set (0.00 sec)

+--------+--------+
| model  | style  |
+--------+--------+
| Boston | Gents  |
| Club   | Gents  |
| Eton   | Gents  |
| Avante | Ladies |
| Denver | Ladies |
+--------+--------+
5 rows in set (0.00 sec)

mysql> _
```

Hot tip

Data retrieved from a column can be sorted by the order of another column whose data is not actually retrieved.

113

Setting direction

By default, **SELECT** queries are automatically sorted in ascending order. An **ORDER BY** clause can explicitly specify the sort direction by adding the keywords **DESC** (descending) or **ASC** (ascending) after the name of the column to sort by, with this syntax:

```
SELECT column-name , column-name
FROM table-name
ORDER BY column-name DESC ;
```

In the SQL script listed below, the **ASC** and **DESC** keywords are used to determine the sort direction for three columns of data.

sort_direction.sql

① Launch a plain text editor, such as Notepad, and create a query defining a table with three columns
```
CREATE TABLE IF NOT EXISTS top_5_films
(
  position      INT PRIMARY KEY ,
  title         CHAR(32) NOT NULL ,
  year          INT NOT NULL
) ;
```

② Next, add a query to insert five records into this table
```
INSERT INTO top_5_films ( position , title , year )
VALUES
( 1 , "Citizen Kane" , 1941 ) ,
( 2 , "Casablanca" , 1942 ) ,
( 3 , "The Godfather" , 1972 ) ,
( 4 , "Gone With The Wind" , 1939 ) ,
( 5 , "Lawrence Of Arabia" , 1962 ) ;
```

③ Now, add a query to display all columns of all records in this table sorted by descending "position" order
```
SELECT * FROM top_5_films ORDER BY position DESC ;
```

④ Add a query to display all years and titles in this table sorted by ascending "year" order
```
SELECT year , title FROM top_5_films ORDER BY year ASC ;
```

⑤ Finally, add a query to display all titles and years in this table sorted by alphabetical "title" order
```
SELECT title , year FROM top_5_films ORDER BY title ASC ;
```

Hot tip

Opinion may be divided on the top five films of all time – the data in this example represents the choice of the American Film Institute.

6 Save the file on your desktop as **sort_direction.sql** then launch the MySQL Command Line Client and issue a query to use the established database
USE site_db ;

7 Now, implement the SQL queries by stating the source path to the SQL file on your system, such as
SOURCE C:\Users\Mike\Desktop\sort_direction.sql

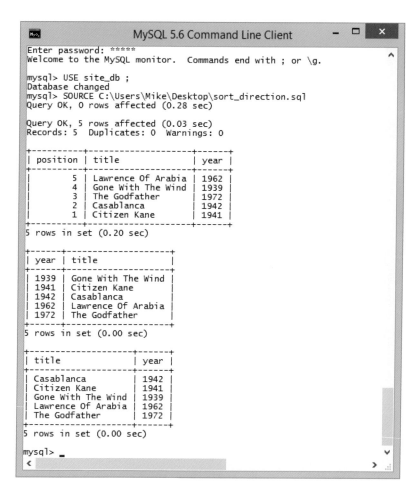

```
                      MySQL 5.6 Command Line Client      –  □  ×

Enter password: *****
Welcome to the MySQL monitor.  Commands end with ; or \g.

mysql> USE site_db ;
Database changed
mysql> SOURCE C:\Users\Mike\Desktop\sort_direction.sql
Query OK, 0 rows affected (0.28 sec)

Query OK, 5 rows affected (0.03 sec)
Records: 5  Duplicates: 0  Warnings: 0

+----------+--------------------+------+
| position | title              | year |
+----------+--------------------+------+
|        5 | Lawrence Of Arabia | 1962 |
|        4 | Gone With The Wind | 1939 |
|        3 | The Godfather      | 1972 |
|        2 | Casablanca         | 1942 |
|        1 | Citizen Kane       | 1941 |
+----------+--------------------+------+
5 rows in set (0.20 sec)

+------+--------------------+
| year | title              |
+------+--------------------+
| 1939 | Gone With The Wind |
| 1941 | Citizen Kane       |
| 1942 | Casablanca         |
| 1962 | Lawrence Of Arabia |
| 1972 | The Godfather      |
+------+--------------------+
5 rows in set (0.00 sec)

+--------------------+------+
| title              | year |
+--------------------+------+
| Casablanca         | 1942 |
| Citizen Kane       | 1941 |
| Gone With The Wind | 1939 |
| Lawrence Of Arabia | 1962 |
| The Godfather      | 1972 |
+--------------------+------+
5 rows in set (0.00 sec)

mysql> _
```

Hot tip

By default, the sort order is not case-sensitive but using **ORDER BY BINARY** gives precedence to uppercase characters in the sort order.

Making comparisons

Like PHP, MySQL has built-in operators and functions that can be used to provide fast filtration of data stored in a database. Using these is highly recommended as it is more efficient than having an SQL query retrieve all data for filtration by PHP. Comparison operators available in MySQL are listed below:

Hot tip

Discover more MySQL built-in features in the MySQL 5.6 Reference Manual online at **dev.mysql.com/doc/refman/5.6**

Operator:	Description:
=	Equality
!=	Inequality
<	Less than
<=	Less than or equal
>	More than
>=	More than or equal
BETWEEN min **AND** max	Within the range min to max
IS NULL	Is a NULL value
IS NOT NULL	Is not a NULL value

Comparison operators are used in a query with a **WHERE** clause to test if a specified condition is met. When the evaluation is **TRUE** the query will return the data, otherwise nothing will be returned.

Usefully, the built-in MySQL **NOW()** function returns the current date and time in the format YYYY-MM-DD HH:MM:SS, which provides a timestamp of when the database was accessed. Additionally, the built-in MySQL **SHA2()** cryptographic hash function allows passwords to be stored securely. This takes two arguments to specify a password and hash string length to return of either 224, 256, 384, or 512 characters.

comparison.sql

1 Launch a plain text editor, such as Notepad, and create a query defining a table with five columns
```
CREATE TABLE IF NOT EXISTS items
(
  id            INT AUTO_INCREMENT PRIMARY KEY ,
  name          CHAR(16)      NOT NULL ,
  quantity      INT           NOT NULL ,
  pass          TEXT(256)     NOT NULL ,
  stamp         DATETIME      NOT NULL
) ;
```

② Next, add a query to insert four records into this table
```
INSERT INTO items ( name , quantity , pass , stamp   )
VALUES  ( "Alan" , 10 , SHA2( "m00nriver", 256) , NOW() ) ,
( "Dean" , 20 , SHA2( "bluem00n", 256 ) ,  NOW() ) ,
( "Gary" , 30 , SHA2( "m00nlight", 256 ) , NOW() ) ,
( "Mike" , 40 ,  SHA2( "m00nshine", 256 ) , NOW() ) ;
```

Don't forget

The timestamp returned by the **NOW()** function will be the current time on the server, which may differ from the local time of the user's timezone.

③ Now, add a query to display names and quantities by comparing "quantity" values
```
SELECT name , quantity FROM items
WHERE quantity BETWEEN 15 AND 35 ;
```

④ Add a query to display one timestamp and checksum
```
SELECT stamp , pass FROM items WHERE quantity < 15 ;
```

⑤ Save the file on your desktop as **comparison.sql** then launch the MySQL Command Line Client and issue a query to use the established database
```
USE site_db ;
```

⑥ Now, implement the SQL queries by stating the source path to the SQL file on your system, such as
```
SOURCE C:\Users\Mike\Desktop\comparison.sql
```

Summary

- Data is inserted into a database table by an **INSERT INTO** query

- The **VALUES** keyword in an **INSERT INTO** query specifies a list of comma-separated values within a single pair of parentheses

- Text data values must be surrounded by quotes

- All data is retrieved from a table with a **SELECT * FROM** query

- All the fields in a column can be changed with an **UPDATE** query

- The **WHERE** keyword can be added to an **UPDATE** query to identify a specific row where a field is to be changed

- The **SET** keyword is used in an **UPDATE** query to change one or more fields in a row

- All the rows in a table can be deleted with a **DELETE** query

- The **WHERE** keyword can be added to a **DELETE** query to identify a specific row that is to be deleted

- All tables should nominate a column to contain a **PRIMARY KEY**

- Multiple column data can be retrieved by stating the column names as a comma-delimited list in a **SELECT** query

- A specific row can be retrieved from a table by adding the **WHERE** keyword to a **SELECT** query to identify the row

- A **WHERE** clause can specify a comma-separated list of alternative comparison values in parentheses following the **IN** keyword

- Data can be returned from rows that do <u>not</u> match any of the list of values by adding a **NOT** keyword before the **IN** keyword

- An **ORDER BY** clause can specify columns to sort by and specify how to sort retrieved data with the **ASC** and **DESC** keywords

- MySQL has comparison operators like those in PHP

- The built-in MySQL **NOW()** function provides a timestamp and the built-in **SHA1()** function stores passwords securely

7 Connecting databases

This chapter demonstrates how to connect to MySQL databases and make SQL queries from PHP scripts.

Making connection

The standard script to connect to the MySQL Server from PHP was described in chapter one when you configured the development environment and is repeated below for explanation:

connect_db.php

```php
<?php
$dbc =
mysqli_connect( 'host' , 'user' , 'password' , 'database' )
OR die ( mysqli_connect_error() ) ;
mysqli_set_charset( $dbc , 'utf-8' ) ;
```

The script defines a PHP variable named "dbc" (database connection) that gets assigned the value returned by the built-in **mysqli_connect()** function. This call requires four arguments to specify the MySQL user details and the database to connect. When the call succeeds, the **mysqli_connect()** function returns an "object" that represents the connection to the MySQL Server.

The object returned by a successful call to **mysqli_connect()** is very important as it is used as an argument in other PHP function calls that communicate with the MySQL Server. For example, in the above script it must be used as the first argument in the call to the **mysqli_set_charset()** function to identify the connection.

When the call to the **mysqli_connect()** function fails, the script branches to an alternative that calls the **die()** function. This is equivalent to calling **exit()** to immediately terminate the script. Optionally, the **die()** function can accept a string argument that will be printed out as the scripts halts. In this case the string message is returned by the **mysqli_connect_error()** function that describes why the connection attempt failed.

As the connection script contains sensitive user details it must not be placed alongside other PHP scripts in your web servers **/htdocs** directory. The **connect_db.php** script should instead be located in the parent directory of **/htdocs** where it is not directly accessible but can be incorporated into other PHP scripts by a **require** statement like this:

require.php

```php
<?php
require ( '../connect_db.php' ) ;

if ( mysqli_ping( $dbc ) )
{
  echo 'MySQL Server ' . mysqli_get_server_info( $dbc ) .
                    ' on ' . mysqli_get_host_info( $dbc ) ;
}
```

The files in your web server's directory structure should therefore be arranged in the hierarchy depicted below so when you request the **require.php** script via HTTP the **connect_db.php** script gets incorporated from its location in the parent directory, and the connection gets made to the MySQL Server.

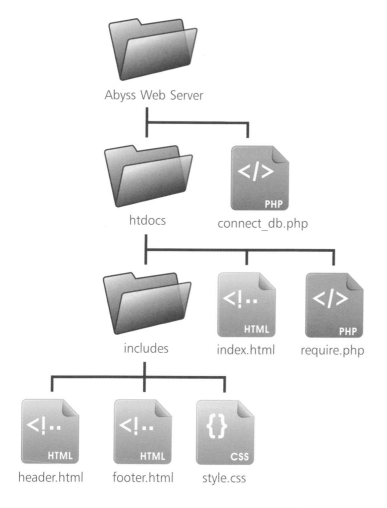

Abyss Web Server

htdocs connect_db.php

includes index.html require.php

header.html footer.html style.css

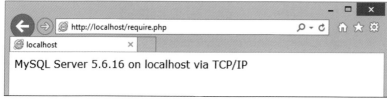

http://localhost/require.php

localhost

MySQL Server 5.6.16 on localhost via TCP/IP

121

Executing queries

Once your PHP script has established a connection to a nominated database on the MySQL Server, queries can be made using the PHP **mysqli_query()** function, which has this syntax:

mysqli_query (*database-connection-object* , *sql-query*)

The database connection object is that assigned to a variable (**$dbc**) by the standard script described on the previous page. Typically, the SQL query is a string assigned to another variable, which can then be used as the second argument to the function.

When the **mysqli_query()** function is called it returns a "result set" or a **TRUE** value where the call is successful, or a **FALSE** value where the call fails. Assigning the returned value to a variable enables the execution of the query to be tested for success or failure.

Optionally, your script can call upon **mysqli_close()** to explicitly close the connection after the query has executed. This will happen automatically at the end of the script anyway but making this call is considered good practice.

query.php

1. Create a PHP script that begins by incorporating the standard script to establish a connection to a database on the MySQL Server

   ```
   <?php

   require ( ' ../connect_db.php ' ) ;
   ```

2. Next, initialize a variable with an SQL query string

   ```
   $q = 'SHOW TABLES' ;
   ```

3. Now, initialize another variable, this time with the result of a query to the database on the MySQL Server

   ```
   $r = mysqli_query ( $dbc , $q ) ;
   ```

4. Test whether the query succeeded and display an appropriate message

   ```
   if ( $r )
   { echo '<h1>Result Set Returned OK</h1>' ; }
   else
   { echo '<p>' . mysqli_error( $dbc ) . '</p>' ; }
   ```

5 Finally, close the MySQL Server database connection
mysqli_close ($dbc) ;

6 Save the PHP script in your web server's **/htdocs** directory
as **query.php** then open it via HTTP to see the message
confirming that the query succeeded

Beware

The SQL query strings
assigned to PHP variables
must not end with a
semi-colon as they must
in the MySQL Command
Line Client.

123

7 Now, edit the SQL query string to make it erroneous
$q = 'SHOW TABLE' ;

8 Save the edited PHP script once more then open it again
via HTTP to see the message describing the query failure

Hot tip

You can make almost
any SQL query using
mysqli_query() that you
can make in the MySQL
Command Line Client.

Retrieving results

Some SQL queries, such as **INSERT**, **UPDATE**, **DELETE** or **ALTER**, return no data from the database so when these are made successfully from a PHP script the **mysqli_query()** function simply returns a **TRUE** value. Other SQL queries, such as **SHOW** or **SELECT**, return a "result set" when made successfully from PHP.

A result set contains rows of records that can be read row-by-row using a **while** loop. Each row can be returned as an array using the **mysqli_fetch_array()** function, which requires the result set variable to be specified as its first argument. Optionally, it may take a second variable to specify what type of array to return – an associative array (using column names), a numeric array, or both. Conveniently, the array type can be specified using one of the built-in PHP constant values listed below:

Constant :	Example:
MYSQLI_ASSOC	$row [*'column-name'*]
MYSQLI_NUM	$row [0]
MYSQLI_BOTH	$row [*'column-name'*] OR $row [0]

Optionally, your script can call upon **mysqli_free_result()** to free the result set resource. This will happen automatically at the end of the script but, as with **mysqli_close()**, making this call is considered good practice.

result.php

1. Create a PHP script that begins by incorporating the standard script to establish a connection to a database on the MySQL Server
```
<?php
require ( ' ../connect_db.php ' ) ;
```

2. Next, initialize a variable with an SQL query string
```
$q = 'SHOW TABLES' ;
```

3. Now, initialize another variable, this time with the result of a query to the database on the MySQL Server
```
$r = mysqli_query ( $dbc , $q ) ;
```

4 Test whether the query succeeded and display an appropriate message

```
if ( $r )
{
  echo '<h1>Tables on site_db database</h1> ' ;
  # Statements to be inserted here (step 5).
}
else
{ echo '<p>' . mysqli_error( $dbc ) . '</p>' ; }
```

5 Now, insert statements to display the data contained in each returned row and free the result set resource

```
while ( $row = mysqli_fetch_array( $r , MYSQLI_NUM ) )
{
  echo '<br>'. $row[ 0 ] ;
}
mysqli_free_result( $r ) ;
```

6 Finally, close the MySQL Server database connection

```
mysqli_close ( $dbc ) ;
```

7 Save the PHP script in your web server's **/htdocs** directory as **result.php** then open it via HTTP to see the result

Don't forget

If the array type is not explicitly specified the **mysqli_fetch_array()** function returns both types by default.

Hot tip

The results shown here list the tables created in the previous two chapters from the MySQL Command Line Client.

125

Applying changes

Changes can be applied to an existing MySQL database table by making SQL queries of **INSERT**, **UPDATE**, **DELETE** or **ALTER**. When these are made from a PHP script by the **mysqli_query()** function it returns a **TRUE** value when the query succeeds. This condition can be tested to perform an appropriate action. For example, to display all records in the table after adding new rows upon success or to display an error message upon failure.

insert.php

1 Create a PHP script that begins by incorporating the standard script to establish a connection to a database on the MySQL Server
```php
<?php
require ( ' ../connect_db.php ' ) ;
```

2 Next, add a function to display all records in an existing table, or display an error message
```php
function show_records( $dbc )
{
  $q = 'SELECT * FROM prints' ;
  $r = mysqli_query( $dbc , $q ) ;

  if ( $r )
  {
    echo '<h1>Records in prints table</h1> ' ;

    while ( $row = mysqli_fetch_array( $r , MYSQLI_ASSOC ) )
    {
      echo '<br>' . $row['id'] . ' | ' . $row[ 'name' ] .
                  ' @ ' . $row[ 'price' ] ;
    }
  }
  else { echo '<p>' . mysqli_error( $dbc ) . '</p>' ; }
}
```

Don't forget

This **SELECT** query uses the **MYSQLI_ASSOC** constant to return the result set as an associative array so the columns can be addressed by name.

3 Now, call the function to display all the records
```php
show_records( $dbc ) ;
```

4 Create and execute another query to add rows to the table
```php
$q = 'INSERT INTO prints ( name , price )
VALUES
( "One Center" , 32.99 ) , ( "Yellow Red Blue" , 36.99 ) ' ;

$r = mysqli_query( $dbc , $q ) ;
```

5 Call the function to display all records again, or display an error message if the change failed

```
if( $r )
{
  show_records( $dbc ) ;
}
else
{
  echo '<p>' . mysqli_error( $dbc ) . '</p>' ;
}
```

6 Finally, close the MySQL Server database connection

```
mysqli_close ( $dbc ) ;
```

7 Save the PHP script in your web server's **/htdocs** directory as **insert.php** then open it via HTTP to see the change to the database table get applied

Counting records

A result set returned by the built-in PHP **mysqli_query()** function can be examined to discover how many rows it contains using the **mysqli_num_rows()** function. This function takes the result set as its argument and returns the number of rows it contains, like this:

```
$num = mysqli_num_rows( $r ) ;
```

Usefully, the returned row count value can be tested before executing the **while** loop that returns records to ensure the result set is not empty.

count.php

1 Create a PHP script that begins by incorporating the standard script to establish a connection to a database on the MySQL Server

```php
<?php
require ( ' ../connect_db.php ' ) ;
```

2 Next, add a function to display all records in an existing table plus the total record count, or an error message

```php
function show_records( $dbc )
{
  $q = 'SELECT * FROM towels' ;
  $r = mysqli_query( $dbc , $q ) ;

  $num = mysqli_num_rows( $r ) ;

  if ( $num > 0 )
  {
    echo '<h1>Records in towels table</h1> ' ;

    while ( $row = mysqli_fetch_array( $r , MYSQLI_ASSOC ) )
    {
      echo '<br>' . $row['name'] . ' | ' . $row[ 'color' ] .
                ' @ ' . $row[ 'price' ] ;
    }
    echo "<br>$num Records" ;
  }
  else { echo '<p>' . mysqli_error( $dbc ) . '</p>' ; }
}
```

3 Now, call the function to display all the records

```php
show_records( $dbc ) ;
```

Hot tip

You can also use the **mysqli_num_rows()** function to paginate results – by displaying a particular number of rows per page.

128

4. Create and execute another query to add a row to the table
```
$q = 'INSERT INTO towels ( name , color , price )
VALUES ( "Sunset" , "Orange" , 9.99 ) ' ;
$r = mysqli_query( $dbc , $q ) ;
```

5. Call the function to display all records again, or display an error message if the change failed
```
if( $r ) { show_records( $dbc ) ; }
else { echo '<p>' . mysqli_error( $dbc ) . '</p>' ; }
```

6. Finally, close the MySQL Server database connection
```
mysqli_close ( $dbc ) ;
```

7. Save the PHP script in your web server's **/htdocs** directory as **count.php** then open it via HTTP to see the change to the database table get applied and the row count change

Hot tip

You can create the original "towels" table from the MySQL Command Line Client by following the steps on page 100.

129

Updating records

The built-in PHP **mysqli_affected_rows()** function returns an integer that is the number of rows affected by an **INSERT**, **UPDATE**, or **DELETE** query. Unlike the **mysqli_num_rows()** function, which takes the result set as its argument, the **mysqli_affected_rows()** function takes the database connection object as its argument:

```
$num_affected = mysqli_affected_rows( $dbc ) ;
```

Usefully, the returned affected row value can be tested to ensure that an **UPDATE** query succeeded on an expected number of records.

update.php

1. Create a PHP script that begins by incorporating the standard script to establish a connection to a database on the MySQL Server
```php
<?php
require ( ' ../connect_db.php ' ) ;
```

2. Next, add a function to display all records in an existing table, or display an error message
```php
function show_records( $dbc )
{
  $q = 'SELECT * FROM watches' ;
  $r = mysqli_query( $dbc , $q ) ;
  $num = mysqli_num_rows( $r ) ;
  if ( $num > 0 )
  {
    echo '<h1>Records in watches table</h1> ' ;
    while ( $row = mysqli_fetch_array( $r , MYSQLI_ASSOC ) )
    {
      echo '<br>' . $row['model'] . ' | ' . $row[ 'style' ] .
                  ' @ ' . $row[ 'price' ] ;
    }
  }
  else { echo '<p>' . mysqli_error( $dbc ) . '</p>' ; }
}
```

Don't forget

Where an **INSERT**, **UPDATE**, or **DELETE** query makes no changes the affected row count will be zero.

3. Now, call the function to display all the records
```php
show_records( $dbc ) ;
```

4. Create and execute another query to update (two) records in the table that have a specified value
```php
$q = 'UPDATE watches
        SET style = "Gents" WHERE style = "Ladies" ' ;
$r = mysqli_query( $dbc , $q ) ;
```

5 Call the function to display all records again if the expected number of records have been updated

```
if( mysqli_affected_rows( $dbc ) == 2 )
{
  echo '<hr>' . mysqli_affected_rows( $dbc ) .
      ' Records Updated...' ;
  show_records( $dbc ) ;
}
```

6 Finally, close the MySQL Server database connection

```
mysqli_close ( $dbc ) ;
```

7 Save the PHP script in your web server's **/htdocs** directory as **update.php** then open it via HTTP to see the change to the database table and the number of affected rows

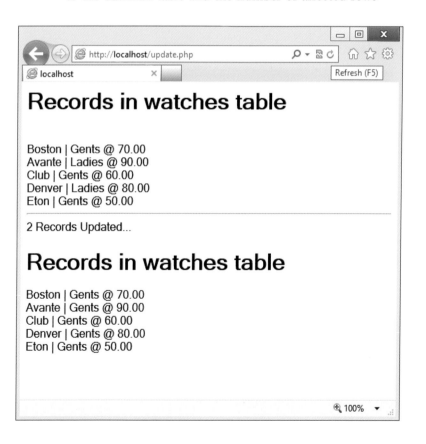

Browser window showing `http://localhost/update.php`:

Records in watches table

Boston | Gents @ 70.00
Avante | Ladies @ 90.00
Club | Gents @ 60.00
Denver | Ladies @ 80.00
Eton | Gents @ 50.00

2 Records Updated...

Records in watches table

Boston | Gents @ 70.00
Avante | Gents @ 90.00
Club | Gents @ 60.00
Denver | Gents @ 80.00
Eton | Gents @ 50.00

Hot tip

You can create the original "watches" table from the MySQL Command Line Client by following the steps on page 112.

Validating results

PHP provides built-in functions that allow data to be tested by type for validation. Each of the functions in the table below return **TRUE** if the data is of a certain type, otherwise they return **FALSE**:

Function :	Validates :	Example :
is_numeric()	Number, even as string	2.0, 20, '20'
is_int()	Integer	100
is_float()	Floating-point number	3.124
is_string()	String	'Hello World!'
is_null()	Null	NULL
is_scalar()	Variable	$var
is_array()	Array	$days
is_bool()	Boolean	TRUE
is_resource()	External Resource	File Stream

validate.php

1 Create a PHP script that begins by incorporating the standard script to establish a connection to a database on the MySQL Server
```php
<?php
require ( ' ../connect_db.php ' ) ;
```

2 Next, add statements to retrieve a single piece of data from a database table for validation
```php
$q =
'SELECT price FROM watches WHERE model = "Boston" ' ;

$r =  mysqli_query( $dbc , $q ) ;

while ( $row = mysqli_fetch_array( $r , MYSQLI_NUM ) )
{ $var = $row[0] ; }
```

③ Now, add statements to test the retrieved data type and
display an appropriate result

```php
$result = is_numeric( $var ) ? 'numeric' : 'not numeric' ;
echo "$var is $result<br>" ;
$result = is_int( $var ) ? 'an integer' : 'not an integer' ;
echo "$var is $result<br>" ;
$result = is_float( $var ) ? 'a float' : 'not a float' ;
echo "$var is $result<br>" ;
$result = is_string( $var ) ? 'a string' : 'not a string' ;
echo "$var is $result<br>" ;
$result = is_null( $var ) ? 'NULL' : 'not NULL' ;
echo "$var is $result<br>" ;
$result = is_scalar( $var ) ? 'a variable' : 'not a variable' ;
echo "$var is $result<br>" ;
$result = is_array( $var ) ? 'an array' : 'not an array' ;
echo "$var is $result<br>" ;
$result = is_bool( $var ) ? 'a boolean' : 'not a boolean' ;
echo "$var is $result<br>" ;
$result = is_resource( $var ) ? 'a resource' : 'not a resource' ;
echo "$var is $result<br>" ;
```

④ Finally, close the MySQL Server database connection
mysqli_close ($dbc) ;

⑤ Save the PHP script in your web server's **/htdocs** directory
as **validate.php** then open it via HTTP to see the results
of the validation tests

Don't forget

You should always
validate data entered by
users into HTML forms
to ensure it is of the
expected data type.

133

Hot tip

You can see here that
the decimal price value is
stored in the variable as
a string, not a float.

Ensuring security

When scripting with PHP and MySQL it is important to consider these security issues to prevent users entering data that may, accidentally or maliciously, produce undesirable effects:

Beware

Removal of HTML tags is especially important as it prevents cross-site scripting (XSS) attacks – by stripping out the **<script>** tags so malicious JavaScript code cannot be executed.

- Do not allow the database connection script to be directly accessible – place it in the parent directory of **/htdocs**

- Employ validation functions to ensure data exists and is of the correct type – frequently use **isset()** , **!empty()** and **is_numeric()**

- Escape special characters in strings to make them safe for queries – first pass them to **mysqli_real_escape_string()**

- Avoid HTML special characters – turn them into entity format with **htmlentities()** or remove them with **strip_tags()**

Allowing users to submit data surrounded by quote marks can cause a script failure when that data gets entered into string, as the quote marks prematurely terminate the string. For example, in the assignment **$str = "Submitted $data"** where the **$data** variable itself contains a string enclosed in quotes. Passing the string to the **mysqli_real_escape_string()** function returns it in a safe format. Similarly, allowing users to submit data surrounded by HTML tags can be problematic but passing it to **strip_tags()** removes the tags, or passing it to **htmlentities()** turns them into entity format.

secure.php

1 Create an HTML document containing a form with one text input field for data submission
```
<form action="secure.php" method="POST">
<p>New Name : <input type="text" name="name">
<input type="submit"></p></form>
```

2 Add a script that displays an item from an existing table
```
<?php
require ( '../connect_db.php' ) ;
# Validation statements to be inserted here (step 3).
$q = 'SELECT * FROM towels WHERE id = 1 ' ;
$r =  mysqli_query( $dbc , $q ) ;
while ( $row = mysqli_fetch_array( $r , MYSQLI_NUM) )
{ echo  "<p>Name : $row[1] </p>" ; }
mysqli_close ( $dbc ) ;
?>
```

3 Next, insert statements to validate the user has submitted
a valid string, then update the existing table record

```
if ( !empty($_POST['name'])  && !is_numeric($_POST['name']) )
{
  $name = $_POST['name'] ;
  # Security statements to be inserted here (step 4).
  $q = 'UPDATE towels SET name= "'.$name.'" WHERE id= 1' ;
  mysqli_query( $dbc , $q ) ;
} else {   echo 'No valid new name submitted' ; }
```

4 Now, insert statements to make the submitted data safe
for use in SQL queries and to remove any HTML tags

```
$name = mysqli_real_escape_string( $dbc , $name ) ;
$name = strip_tags( $name ) ;
```

5 Save the PHP script in your web server's **/htdocs** directory
as **secure.php** then open it via HTTP and submit data
enclosed in HTML tags and quote marks to see them
securely handled by the script

Hot tip

You can comment out
(by inserting a # at the
beginning of the line)
the first statement in
step 4 to see the update
fail, or comment out its
second statement to see
the update then display
in a bold font.

135

Hot tip

You can create the
original "towels"
table from the MySQL
Command Line Client by
following the steps on
page 100.

Handling errors

PHP provides useful error messages when it encounters problems with a script – describing both runtime and syntax errors. Additionally, you can create your own custom error handler to provide messages describing script problems that may arise.

Each error that occurs can be defined by a built-in PHP constant that has a unique numerical value, like those in the table below:

Value :	Constant :	Description :
1	E_ERROR	Fatal runtime error, which halts execution of the script
2	E_WARNING	Non-fatal runtime error, which does not halt the script
4	E_PARSE	Syntax error, which prevents the interpreter running the script
8	E_NOTICE	Possible runtime error, which simply provides a notice tip
256	E_USER_ERROR	Fatal user-generated error, set by the trigger_error() function
512	E_USER_WARNING	Non-fatal user-generated error, set by trigger_error() function
1024	E_USER_NOTICE	User-generated notice, set by the trigger_error() function

Hot tip

PHP error handling is set on by its configuration file, but can also be set on manually by calling **ini_set('display_errors',1)**.

A custom error handler function of your own name is nominated as the argument to the PHP **set_error_handler()** function. Errors generate five descriptive components that can be passed as arguments to your error handler – error level, message, file, line, and context. The error level and message are mandatory.

In scripts that handle user input it is useful to "trigger" errors when the user enters inappropriate data. This is achieved using the PHP **trigger_error()** function, which takes two arguments to specify the error message and level. As this function only describes user-generated errors the specified error level must be one of the **E_USER** constant types in the table above.

1 Create an HTML document containing a PHP script that begins by nominating a custom error handler function

```php
<?php
set_error_handler( 'error_handler' ) ;
```

error.php

2 Next, add the custom error handler function to display error details to the user when called

```php
function error_handler ( $level , $message , $file , $line )
{
  echo "Error [$level] : $message <br>
                (Check line $line in $file )"  ;
}
```

3 Now, initialize a variable, simulating a user input value

```php
$num = 500 ;
```

4 Finally, set the trigger to call the custom error handler

```php
if ( $num > 100 )
{  trigger_error( 'Number must be less than 100' ,
                            E_USER_ERROR ) ; }

?>
```

5 Save the PHP script in your web server's **/htdocs** directory as **error.php** then open it via HTTP to see the message generated by your custom error handler function

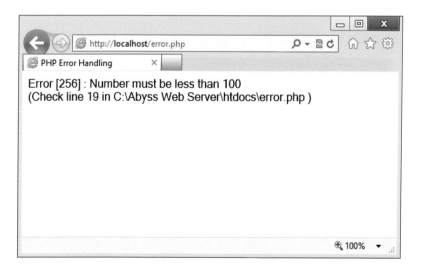

Hot tip

Individual expression errors can be supressed by prefixing the expression with the @ error control operator. So **$num = @(8 / 0) ;** suppresses the default Division By Zero error message.

Summary

- The PHP **mysqli_connect()** function connects a user to a specified database and returns a database connection object

- A database connection object is used as an argument in other PHP functions that communicate with the database

- The PHP **mysqli_query()** function sends SQL queries to the connected database on the MySQL Server

- When the **mysqli_query()** function is called it returns a result set or a **TRUE** value upon success, or a **FALSE** value upon failure

- Optionally, **mysqli_close()** can be called to explicitly close the database connection

- An SQL **SELECT** query returns a result set that contains rows of records that can be read row-by-row using a **while** loop

- The PHP **mysqli_fetch_array()** function returns each row of a result set as an associative or numbered array

- Optionally, **mysqli_free_result()** can be called to explicitly free a result set resource

- An SQL **INSERT, UPDATE, DELETE,** or **ALTER** query simply returns a **TRUE** value upon success

- The PHP **mysqli_num_rows()** function returns an integer that is the number of rows within a specified result set

- The **mysqli_affected_rows()** function returns an integer that is the number of rows affected by an **INSERT, UPDATE,** or **DELETE**

- PHP functions that test data by type return **TRUE** if the data is of a certain type, otherwise they return **FALSE**

- The **mysqli_real_escape_string()** function escapes special characters from strings and **strip_tags()** removes HTML tags

- The **set_error_handler()** function nominates a custom error handler and **trigger_error()** can be used to generate errors

8 Registering users

This chapter demonstrates how to create a simple registration procedure and login application.

Creating a users database

User details can be usefully stored in a MySQL database table upon their first registration visit so those details may be easily retrieved upon subsequent visits for comparison by a PHP script. When the user enters login details matching those already stored in the database table the script can allow access to the website. Typically, a database table containing user details might store the user ID, first name, last name, email address, password, and registration date of each user in individual columns:

Column Name:	Content Type:	Example:
user_id	Number	123
first_name	Text	Mike
last_name	Text	McGrath
email	Text	mike@example.com
pass	Text	m00nshine
reg_date	Date/Time	2013-02-14 12:30:00

Don't forget

MySQL database tables can only be created by the root MySQL user or other MySQL user that has been granted full access privileges.

The design of this database table simply requires **CHAR** or **VARCHAR** data types to be specified for those columns storing text. User IDs should be positive (**UNSIGNED**) integer **INT** values that the table automatically allocates with **AUTO_INCREMENT**, and the user's first registration timestamp stored as a **DATETIME** value. The user's email address should be **UNIQUE**, so they cannot be registered more than once, and as all these items will be required for registration each column must have a **NOT NULL** rule.

The SQL command required to produce this design as a MySQL database table named "users" can be issued at the prompt in the MySQL Command Line Client. Alternatively, the SQL command can be saved in an SQL file, which can be implemented at the MySQL Command Line Client prompt by issuing the **SOURCE** command followed by the path to the SQL file on your system.

...cont'd

① Launch a plain text editor and create an SQL command describing the table requirements shown opposite
CREATE TABLE IF NOT EXISTS users (
user_id INT UNSIGNED NOT NULL AUTO_INCREMENT ,
first_name VARCHAR(20) NOT NULL ,
last_name VARCHAR(40) NOT NULL ,
email VARCHAR(60) NOT NULL ,
pass CHAR(40) NOT NULL ,
reg_date DATETIME NOT NULL ,
PRIMARY KEY (user_id) ,
UNIQUE (email)) ;

create_users.sql

② Save the file as **create_users.sql** then launch the MySQL Command Line Client and log in as a user with full access privileges, such as the root user

③ Next, issue a command to use the established database
USE site_db ;

④ Now, implement the SQL command by stating the source path to the SQL file on your system, such as
SOURCE C:\Users\Mike\Desktop\create_users.sql

⑤ Finally, issue a command to confirm the table format
EXPLAIN users ;

141

Beware

Name the users password column 'pass' rather than 'password' – to avoid confusion with the built-in MySQL **password()** function.

Providing a register page

A user registration form might typically provide input fields requiring the user to input their first name, last name, email address, and a unique password. This can be displayed on a web page by a PHP script that also includes page header and footers.

```
http://localhost/register.php

Register                    ×

Page Header

Register

First Name: [        ]        Last Name: [          ]

Email Address: [                              ]

Password: [          ]      Confirm Password: [        ]

[ Register ]

Page Footer

                                        100%
```

Don't forget

The page's header and footer are included HTML documents simply styled by a CSS stylesheet.

The PHP script can also process the form when submitted to first ensure the user has entered valid data in each field, then insert that user data into the MySQL database "users" table created on the previous page.

In order to process the form, the HTML **<form>** tag's **method** attribute should specify the form be submitted using the **POST** method and its **action** method should specify the name of the same PHP script that displays the form. This allows any input entered by the user to be retained by the input fields in the event that any item fails validation.

When the form is submitted after user input, the PHP script will display messages to advise the user of any validation error or display a confirmation that registration has succeeded and provide a hyperlink to a login page.

① Launch a plain text editor and begin a PHP script with statements to set the page title and include a page header
```php
<?php

$page_title = 'Register' ;
include ( 'includes/header.html' ) ;
```

register.php

② Now, add a conditional test that will only execute the statements it contains if the form has been submitted
```php
if ( $_SERVER[ 'REQUEST_METHOD' ] == 'POST' )
{
    # Statements to be inserted here (steps 3-10).
}
?>
```

Don't forget

The database connection variable **$dbc** is intialized by the **connect_db.php** script and the **$_POST[]** array contains the values in the named form fields.

③ Next, insert statements to open the database connection and initialize an array for error messages
```php
require ( '../connect_db.php' ) ;
$errors = array() ;
```

④ Insert statements to store an error message if the first name field remains empty, or store its value in a variable
```php
if ( empty( $_POST[ 'first_name' ] ) )
{ $errors[] = 'Enter your first name.' ; }
else
{ $fn = mysqli_real_escape_string( $dbc,
                    trim( $_POST[ 'first_name' ] ) ) ; }
```

⑤ Now, insert statements to store an error message if the last name field remains empty, or store its value in a variable
```php
if ( empty( $_POST[ 'last_name' ] ) )
{ $errors[] = 'Enter your last name.' ; }
else
{ $ln = mysqli_real_escape_string( $dbc,
                    trim( $_POST[ 'last_name' ] ) ) ; }
```

Hot tip

Use the **mysqli_real_escape_string()** function to escape special characters and the **trim()** function to remove unwanted spaces.

⑥ Insert statements to store an error message if the email address field remains empty, or store its value in a variable
```php
if ( empty( $_POST[ 'email' ] ) )
{ $errors[] = 'Enter your email address.' ; }
else
{ $e = mysqli_real_escape_string( $dbc,
                    trim( $_POST[ 'email' ] ) ) ; }
```

143

...cont'd

7 Next, insert statements to store the password value in a variable if the passwords are a valid match, or store an error message if they do not match or the first field is empty

```php
if ( !empty( $_POST[ 'pass1' ] ) )
{
  if ( $_POST[ 'pass1' ] != $_POST[ 'pass2' ] )
  { $errors[] = 'Passwords do not match.' ; }
  else
  { $p = mysqli_real_escape_string( $dbc,
                          trim( $_POST[ 'pass1' ] ) ) ; }
}
else { $errors[] = 'Enter your password.' ; }
```

8 Insert statements to store an error message if the email address is already registered in the 'users' database table

```php
if ( empty( $errors ) )
{
  $q = "SELECT user_id FROM users WHERE email='$e'" ;
  $r = mysqli_query ( $dbc , $q ) ;
  if ( mysqli_num_rows( $r ) != 0 )
  { $errors[] = 'Email address already registered.
                    <a href="login.php">Login</a>' ; }
}
```

9 Now, insert statements to store the user data in the database table, display a confirmation when registration succeeds, close the database connection, include a page footer, and exit the script

```php
if ( empty( $errors ) )
{
  $q = "INSERT INTO users
          (first_name, last_name, email, pass, reg_date)
          VALUES ('$fn', '$ln', '$e', SHA1('$p'), NOW() )" ;
  $r = mysqli_query ( $dbc , $q ) ;

  if ( $r )
  {
    echo '<h1>Registered!</h1>
          <p>You are now registered.</p>
          <p><a href="login.php">Login</a></p>' ;
  }

  mysqli_close( $dbc ) ;
  include ( 'includes/footer.html' ) ;
  exit() ;
}
```

10 Append alternative statements to display all stored error messages when registration cannot be completed and close the database connection

```
else
{
  echo '<h1>Error!</h1>
  <p id="err_msg">The following error(s) occurred:<br>' ;
  foreach ( $errors as $msg )
  {
    echo " - $msg<br>" ;
  }
  echo 'Please try again.</p>' ;
  mysqli_close( $dbc ) ;
}
```

Beware

Always remember to close the database connection when access is no longer needed.

11 Now, add the HTML sticky form that uses this script

```
<h1>Register</h1>
<form action="register.php" method="POST">
<p>
First Name: <input type="text" name="first_name"
value="<?php if ( isset( $_POST[ 'first_name' ] ) )
        echo $_POST[ 'first_name' ] ; ?>">
Last Name: <input type="text" name="last_name"
value="<?php if ( isset( $_POST[ 'last_name' ] ) )
        echo $_POST[ 'last_name' ] ; ?>">
</p> <p>
Email Address: <input type="text" name="email"
value="<?php if ( isset( $_POST[ 'email' ] ) )
        echo $_POST[ 'email' ] ; ?>">
</p> <p>
Password: <input type="password" name="pass1"
value="<?php if ( isset( $_POST[ 'pass1' ] ) )
        echo $_POST[ 'pass1' ] ; ?>" >
Confirm Password: <input type="password" name="pass2"
value="<?php if ( isset( $_POST[ 'pass2' ] ) )
        echo $_POST[ 'pass2' ] ; ?>">
</p> <p>
<input type="submit" value="Register"> </p>
</form>
```

Hot tip

Assign the values passed to the **$_POST[]** global variable array upon submission to retain the field values when registration fails.

12 Add a final script instruction to include a page footer then save the script in your web server's **/htdocs** directory as **register.php**

```
<?php include ( 'includes/footer.html' ) ; ?>
```

Processing registrations

Having created the user registration page, described on the previous pages, you can now test the registration process to ensure the validation checks perform correctly and the PHP script provides appropriate confirmation messages to the user.

1 With the MySQL Server running, enter the location **http://localhost/register.php** into your web browser's address field to see Abyss serve up the registration page

2 Now click the "Register" button to see messages appear advising that field validation has failed for each input

3 Next, complete all input fields ensuring you enter identical password values, then click the "Register" button once more to see a message advising that registration has succeeded and providing a hyperlink to a login page

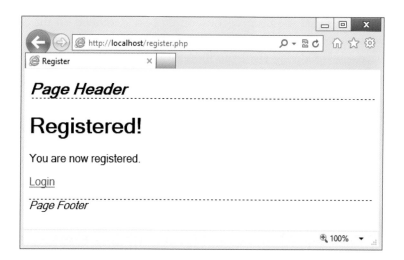

Try entering differing password values to see registration fail with a message advising that passwords do not match.

4 Return to the registration page and enter identical user details as before, then click the "Register" button to see a message appear advising that your email address is registered and providing a hyperlink to a login page

Remember that the MySQL Server must be running so the input data can be written into the users table for subsequent comparison.

Providing a login page

Having completed the user registration process, described on the previous pages, you can now create the login page that the user can access by following the hyperlinks provided upon registration, or by addressing the login page directly.

login.php

1 Launch a plain text editor and begin a PHP script with statements to set the page title and include a page header

```php
<?php

$page_title = 'Login' ;
include ( 'includes/header.html' ) ;
```

2 Now, add a conditional test that will display any error messages if they exist and provide a hyperlink back to the registration page when the login attempt fails

```php
if ( isset( $errors ) && !empty( $errors ) )
{
  echo '<p id="err_msg">Oops! There was a problem:<br>' ;
  foreach ( $errors as $msg )
  {
    echo " - $msg<br>" ;
  }
  echo 'Please try again or
          <a href="register.php">Register</a></p>' ;
}
?>
```

The **$errors** array will only be set by the PHP handler script after the form has been submitted when login fails.

3 Next, add the HTML form that will submit the user login details to be processed by a PHP script

```html
<h1>Login</h1>
<form action="login_action.php" method="POST">
<p>
Email Address: <input type="text" name="email">
</p><p>
Password: <input type="password" name="pass">
</p><p>
<input type="submit" value="Login" >
</p>
</form>
```

4 Add a final script instruction to include a page footer then save the script in your web server's **/htdocs** directory as **login.php**

```php
<?php include ( 'includes/footer.html' ) ; ?>
```

5 Click the hyperlink on the registration page or enter the location **http://localhost/login.php** into your web browser's address field to see Abyss serve up the login page

> http://localhost/login.php
>
> Login ×
>
> ### *Page Header*
> --------------------------------
>
> # Login
>
> Email Address: [_____]
>
> Password: [_____]
>
> [Login]
> --------------------------------
> *Page Footer*
>
> 🔍 100% ▼

Beware

Clicking the Login button before the PHP handler script has been created will simply produce an HTTP404 Page Not Found error.

149

When the login form is submitted, a validation function must ensure the fields are not empty then seek their input values in the "users" database table.

If the submitted values are found, the login attempt succeeds so the corresponding user id, first name, and last name, can be retrieved from the "users" table and a further function can be called to load a home page in the browser.

If the submitted values are not found, the login attempt fails and the validation function will simply set a descriptive error message.

These two functions, to validate form fields and to load a new page, can usefully be created as login "tools" within an independent PHP script so they may be readily called from the script nominated to handle the login page form and by other PHP scripts as the user navigates to other pages in the website.

Hot tip

Create functions in independent PHP scripts for modularity if they can be useful to multiple pages across a website.

Supplying login tools

Having completed the user login form, described on the previous pages, you can now create the login tools that will validate login attempts and load a new page when required. These tools can be easily made available to other pages on the website simply by inserting in them a PHP **require** statement naming this script.

login_tools.php

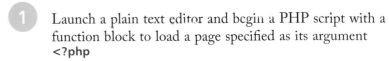 Launch a plain text editor and begin a PHP script with a function block to load a page specified as its argument

```php
<?php
function load( $page = 'login.php' )
{
  # Statements to be inserted here (steps 2-4).
}
```

Hot tip

Assign the name of the login page to the load argument to become the default page to load if no other page is specified by the caller.

150

 Now, in the load function block, insert a statement to build a URL string of protocol, current domain, and directory

```php
$url = 'http://' . $_SERVER[ 'HTTP_HOST' ] .
              dirname( $_SERVER[ 'PHP_SELF' ] ) ;
```

3 Next, in the load function block, insert statements to remove any trailing slashes from the URL string, then append a forward slash and the specified page argument

```php
$url = rtrim( $url , '/\' ) ;
$url .= '/' . $page ;
```

Don't forget

The existence of a sub-directory may add trailing slashes to the URL string so these must be removed before appending the page.

4 Finally, in the load function block, insert statements to load the specified page then quit the script

```php
header( "Location: $url" ) ;
exit() ;
```

 Add a function block to validate the user login details as correct or supply error messages

```php
function validate( $dbc , $email = '' , $pwd = '' )
{
  # Statements to be inserted here (steps 6-10).
}
```

6 In the validate function block insert a statement to initialize an array for error messages

```php
$errors = array() ;
```

7 Next, insert statements to store an error message if the email field remains empty, or store its value in a variable

```
if ( empty( $email ) )
{ $errors[] = 'Enter your email address.' ; }
else
{ $e = mysqli_real_escape_string( $dbc , trim( $email ) ) ; }
```

8 Now, insert statements to store an error message if the password field remains empty, or store its value in a variable

```
if ( empty( $pwd ) )
{ $errors[] = 'Enter your password.' ; }
else
{ $p = mysqli_real_escape_string( $dbc , trim( $pwd ) ) ; }
```

9 Insert statements to store an error message if the email and password are not found in the database table, or return the associated user id, first name, and last name to the caller – if the login attempt succeeds

```
if ( empty( $errors ) )
{
  $q = "SELECT user_id, first_name, last_name
        FROM users
        WHERE email = '$e'
        AND pass = SHA1( '$p' ) " ;

  $r = mysqli_query ( $dbc , $q ) ;

  if ( mysqli_num_rows( $r ) == 1 )
  {
    $row = mysqli_fetch_array ( $r , MYSQLI_ASSOC ) ;
    return array( true , $row ) ;
  }
  else
  { $errors[] = 'Email address and password not found.' ; }
}
```

10 Finally, insert a statement in the validate function block to return the list of error messages to the caller – if the login attempt fails

```
return array( false , $errors ) ;    }
```

11 Be sure to now save this script in your web server's **/htdocs** directory as **login_tools.php**

Hot tip

For stability you should use the **mysqli_ real_escape_string()** function to escape any unexpected characters.

Beware

The registration process stored the user password in encrypted format using the MySQL **SHA1()** function (see page 116) – so the SELECT comparison must also use that function.

151

Processing login attempts

Having completed the login form and the login tools, described on the previous pages, you can now create the PHP script to actually process login attempts. When a login attempt succeeds, this script will set user details retrieved from the database as session data – so the logged-in user can be easily recognized as they navigate between other pages of the same website.

login_action.php

① Launch a plain text editor and begin a PHP script with a test block to see if the login form has been submitted
```php
<?php

if ( $_SERVER[ 'REQUEST_METHOD' ] == 'POST' )
{
    # Statements to be inserted here (steps 2-6).
}
```

② Now, insert a statement to open the database connection
```php
require ( '../connect_db.php' ) ;
```

③ Next, insert a statement to make the login tools available
```php
require ( 'login_tools.php' ) ;
```

④ Insert a statement to ensure login succeeded and get the associated user details of id, first name, and last name
```php
list ( $check , $data ) =
    validate ( $dbc , $_POST[ 'email' ] , $_POST[ 'pass' ] ) ;
```

⑤ Now, insert statements to set the user details as session data and load a home page, or assign error messages
```php
if ( $check )
{
    session_start() ;

    $_SESSION[ 'user_id' ] = $data[ 'user_id' ] ;
    $_SESSION[ 'first_name' ] = $data[ 'first_name' ] ;
    $_SESSION[ 'last_name' ] = $data[ 'last_name' ] ;

    load ( 'home.php' ) ;
}
else { $errors = $data ; }
```

⑥ Next, insert a statement to close the database connection
```php
mysqli_close( $dbc ) ;
```

7 Finally, after the test block, add a statement to continue display of the login page when the login attempt fails
include ('login.php') ;

8 Save this script in your web server's **/htdocs** directory as **login_action.php** then enter the login page location **http://localhost/login.php** in your web browser's address field and attempt to login with incorrect user details

Beware

This login form is not a "sticky" form – so the entered user details are not retained after the form gets submitted.

153

Hot tip

The **validate()** function in **login_tools.php** sets the error message shown here – so it gets displayed by **login.php** when loaded by the include statement in **login_action.php**.

Confirming login success

Having completed the PHP script to actually process login attempts, described on the previous pages, you can now create the home page to be loaded when the login attempt succeeds. Typically, this will contain hyperlinks to allow the user to navigate between other pages of the website.

home.php

1 Launch a plain text editor and begin a PHP script with a statement to allow access to session data
```
<?php

session_start() ;
```

2 Now, add statements to redirect the browser to the login page if the user is not already logged in
```
if ( !isset( $_SESSION[ 'user_id' ] ) )
{
  require ( 'login_tools.php' ) ;
  load() ;
}
```

3 Next, add statements to set the page title and include a page header
```
$page_title = 'Home' ;

include ( 'includes/header.html' ) ;
```

Don't forget

The home page cannot be reached until completing the login process during which the session variable gets set.

4 Add a statement to confirm the named user is logged in
```
echo "<h1>HOME</h1>
<p>You are now logged in,
{ $_SESSION[ 'first_name' ] } { $_SESSION[ 'last_name' ] }
</p>" ;
```

5 Now, add statements to create hyperlinks to other pages on this website
```
echo '<p>
<a href="forum.php">Forum</a> |
<a href="shop.php">Shop</a> |
<a href="goodbye.php">Logout</a>
</p> ' ;
```

6 Add a final statement to include a page footer
```
include ( 'includes/footer.html' ) ;

?>
```

7 Save this script in your web server's **/htdocs** directory as **home.php** then enter the login page location **http://localhost/login.php** in your web browser's address field and attempt to login with correct user details

Hot tip

The hyperlinks on the home page will be used to demonstrate PHP forums and e-commerce in the following two chapters of this book.

Summary

- User details can be stored in a MySQL database table for comparison on subsequent visits to a website

- Typically, a MySQL database users table might store their id, names, email address, password, and date of registration

- A typical registration form might request the user's names, their email address, and their chosen password twice

- The registration form should be submitted by the **POST** method and specify the name of a PHP script as its action

- The PHP script processing a registration attempt should first ensure that all required field data is valid and provide appropriate error message where validation fails

- When all registration data appears valid the PHP script processing a registration attempt can then store the submitted user data in a MySQL database users table

- A typical login form might request the user's email address and the password chosen by them during the registration process

- The login form should be submitted by the **POST** method and specify the name of a PHP script as its action

- Login tools can be contained in a separate PHP script so they can be easily made available to other pages on the website

- The PHP script processing a login attempt should ensure that all required field data is valid and that the user exists in the users database, or provide an appropriate error message

- When all login data is valid and the user found in the database the PHP script processing a login attempt can store the user details as session data so the user can be easily recognized as they navigate between other pages on that website

- The PHP script processing a successful login attempt can load the website's home page containing navigation links

9 Providing forums

This chapter builds on the previous chapter to demonstrate how to create a simple forum application.

Creating a forum database

User messages can be stored in a MySQL database table by a PHP script so they may be subsequently retrieved for display in a forum page containing messages from various registered users. Typically, a database table containing posted user messages might store the post ID, the user's first name and last name, the subject title, the message itself, and the date when posted:

Column Name:	Content Type:	Example:
post_id	Number	123
first_name	Text	Mike
last_name	Text	McGrath
subject	Text	Ice Cream
message	Text	Delicious on a hot day.
post_date	Date/Time	2014-02-14 12:30:00

The design of this database table simply requires that **VARCHAR** or **TEXT** data types should be specified for those columns storing text. Post IDs should be positive (**UNSIGNED**) integer **INT** values that the table automatically allocates with **AUTO_INCREMENT**, and the message posted timestamp should be stored as a **DATETIME** value. All these items will be required to post a message to the database table so each column must have a **NOT NULL** rule.

The SQL command required to produce this design as a MySQL database table named "forum" can be issued at the prompt in the MySQL Command Line Client. Alternatively, the SQL command can be saved in an SQL file, which can be implemented at the MySQL Command Line Client prompt by issuing the **SOURCE** command followed by the path to the SQL file on your system.

Don't forget

MySQL database tables can only be created by the root MySQL user or other MySQL user that has been granted full access privileges.

1 Launch a plain text editor and create an SQL command describing the table requirements shown opposite
CREATE TABLE IF NOT EXISTS forum (
post_id INT UNSIGNED NOT NULL AUTO_INCREMENT ,
first_name VARCHAR(20) NOT NULL ,
last_name VARCHAR(40) NOT NULL ,
subject VARCHAR(60) NOT NULL ,
message TEXT NOT NULL ,
post_date DATETIME NOT NULL ,
PRIMARY KEY (post_id)) ;

create_forum.sql

2 Save the file as **create_forum.sql** then launch the MySQL Command Line Client and log in as a user with full access privileges, such as the root user

3 Next, issue a command to use the established database
USE site_db ;

4 Now, implement the SQL command by stating the source path to the SQL file on your system, such as
SOURCE C:\Users\Mike\Desktop\create_forum.sql

5 Finally, issue a command to confirm the table format
EXPLAIN users ;

Hot tip

The MySQL **TEXT** data type accommodates up to 65,535 characters. Larger messages can be accommodated with **MEDIUMTEXT** and **LONGTEXT** data types.

Providing a forum page

Typically, a message board page displaying posted forum messages might only be available to registered users. The PHP script providing this page can check that the user is registered by testing the session data and redirect to the login page when this test fails. When the test succeeds, previous posted messages can be retrieved from the MySQL forum database table for display on the page or the script can simply advise that there are currently no messages. Forum messages can be displayed between page header and footers together with a hyperlink to another page where the current user can post a new forum message.

forum.php

1 Launch a plain text editor and begin a PHP script with a statement to allow access to session data
```php
<?php

session_start() ;
```

2 Now, add statements to redirect the browser to the login page if the user is not already logged in
```php
if ( !isset( $_SESSION[ 'user_id' ] ) )
{
  require ( 'login_tools.php' ) ;
  load() ;
}
```

Don't forget

The forum page cannot be reached until completing the login process during which the session variable gets set.

3 Next, add statements to set the page title and include a page header
```php
$page_title = 'Forum' ;
include ( 'includes/header.html' ) ;
```

4 Add a statement to open the database connection
```php
require ( '..\connect_db.php' ) ;
```

5 Now, add statements to retrieve messages from the database or provide a default message
```php
$q = "SELECT * FROM forum" ;
$r = mysqli_query( $dbc , $q ) ;
if ( mysqli_num_rows( $r ) > 0 )
{
  # Statements to be inserted here (step 6).
}
else
{ echo '<p>There are currently no messages.</p>' ; }
```

6 Next, insert statements to write a table displaying all messages retrieved from the database table if any found

```
echo '<table><tr><th>Posted By</th>
<th>Subject</th><th id="msg">Message</th></tr>';
while ( $row = mysqli_fetch_array( $r , MYSQLI_ASSOC ) )
{
  echo '<tr>
  <td>'.$row['first_name'].' '.$row['last_name'].'<br>'
                              .$row['post_date'].'</td>
  <td>'.$row['subject'].'</td><td>'.$row['message'].'</td>
  </tr>';
}
echo '</table>' ;
```

Don't forget

The cells on a table row will be populated by the data contained in the columns on a row of the database forum table.

7 Add a statement to create hyperlinks to other pages on this website, including a "Post Message" page

```
echo '<p>
<a href="post.php">Post Message</a> |
<a href="shop.php">Shop</a> |
<a href="home.php">Home</a> |
<a href="goodbye.php">Logout</a></p>' ;
```

8 Now, add a statement to close the database connection

```
mysqli_close( $dbc ) ;
```

9 Add a final statement to include a page footer

```
include ( 'includes/footer.html' ) ;          ?>
```

10 Save this script in your web brower's **/htdocs** directory as **forum.php** then log in and follow the link on the home page to the forum

Hot tip

The hyperlinks on the forum page will be used to demonstrate PHP e-commerce and allow the user to post a message, return to the home page, or log out.

161

Supplying a message form

Having completed the PHP script to display posted forum messages, described on the previous pages, you can now create a PHP script to allow the user to post new messages. This can check that the user is indeed logged in then simply provide a form with fields for the subject title and the message body itself.

PHP

post.php

1. Launch a plain text editor and begin a PHP script with a statement to allow access to session data
```
<?php

session_start() ;
```

2. Now, add statements to redirect the browser to the login page if the user is not already logged in
```
if ( !isset( $_SESSION[ 'user_id' ] ) )
{
  require ( 'login_tools.php' ) ;
  load() ;
}
```

3. Next, add statements to set the page title and include a page header
```
$page_title = 'Post Message' ;
include ( 'includes/header.html' ) ;
```

Hot tip

Notice that the form **action** attribute nominates a submission handler named **post_action.php** – this is listed on pages 164-5.

4. Add a statement to display the form
```
echo '<form action="post_action.php" method="POST"
                              accept-charset="utf-8">
<p>Subject:<br>
<input name="subject" type="text" size="64"></p>
<p>Message:<br>
<textarea name="message" rows="5" cols="50">
</textarea></p>
<p><input type="submit" value="Submit"></p>
</form>' ;
```

5. Next, add a statement to create hyperlinks to other pages on this website
```
echo '<p>
<a href="forum.php">Forum</a> |
<a href="shop.php">Shop</a> |
<a href="home.php">Home</a> |
<a href="goodbye.php">Logout</a></p>' ;
```

6 Add a final statement to include a page footer
include ('includes/footer.html') ; **?>**

7 Save this script in your web brower's **/htdocs** directory as
post.php then log in and follow the link on the forum
page to this post message page

Don't forget

This page provides a
hyperlink back to the
Forum page, should the
user wish to return there.

Processing posted messages

Having completed the PHP script to supply a form to post new forum messages, described on the previous pages, you can now create a PHP script to process the submitted messages. This can check that the user is logged in then ensure that the subject and message fields are not empty. Once the form input is found to be valid the script can then store the submitted message in the MySQL "forum" database table. If the attempt to post the message succeeds the forum page can be loaded to display the messages, or upon failure an error message can be displayed:

post_action.php

1 Launch a plain text editor and begin a PHP script with a statement to allow access to session data
```php
<?php

session_start() ;
```

2 Next, add a statement to make the load function available
```php
require ( 'login_tools.php' ) ;
```

3 Now, add a statement to redirect the browser to the login page if the user is not already logged in
```php
if ( !isset( $_SESSION[ 'user_id' ] ) ) { load() ; }
```

4 Add statements to set the page title and include a page header
```php
$page_title = 'Post Error' ;
include ( 'includes/header.html' ) ;
```

Don't forget

This script is nominated by the form in **post.php** to process its submitted user data messages.

5 Next, add a statements block to ensure the submitted form fields are not empty, or display an error message
```php
if ( $_SERVER[ 'REQUEST_METHOD' ] == 'POST' )
{
  if ( empty( $_POST[ 'subject'] ) )
  { echo '<p>Please enter a subject for this post.</p>' ; }

  if ( empty( $_POST[ 'message' ] ) )
  { echo '<p>Please enter a message for this post.</p>'; }

  # Statements to be inserted here (step 6).

}
```

6 Insert into the block statements to add the form data to the MySQL "forum" database table

```
if( !empty( $_POST[ 'subject' ] )
                    && !empty( $_POST[ 'message'] ) )
{
  require ( '../connect_db.php' ) ;
  $q = "INSERT INTO forum
        (first_name,last_name,subject,message,post_date)
        VALUES (
        '{$_SESSION[first_name]}' ,
        '{$_SESSION[last_name]}' ,
        '{$_POST[subject]}' ,
        '{$_POST[message]}' ,
        NOW() )" ;
  $r = mysqli_query ( $dbc , $q ) ;

  # Statements to be inserted here (step 7).

  mysqli_close( $dbc ) ;
}
```

Hot tip

This script supplies its own error messages if it finds empty form fields or a MySQL error message if the data cannot be added to the database table.

7 Now, insert statements to display the forum messages on success, or display a MySQL error message on failure

```
if ( mysqli_affected_rows( $dbc ) != 1 )
{
  echo '<p>Error</p>'.mysqli_error( $dbc ) ;
}
else
{
  load( 'forum.php' ) ;
}
```

Beware

The form is not sticky so field data is not retained.

8 After the statements block, add a statement to create a hyperlink back to the forum page

```
echo '<p><a href="forum.php">Forum</a>' ;
```

9 Add a final statement to include a page footer

```
include ( 'includes/footer.html' ) ;          ?>
```

10 Save this script in your web brower's **/htdocs** directory as **post_action.php** then submit the form with no subject or message to see the script display error messages

Confirming post success

Having created the PHP script to process submitted forum messages, described on the previous pages, you can now test the message board process to ensure the validation checks perform correctly to display errors when appropriate, and that posted messages appear on the forum page.

 Log in and navigate to the Post Message page, then enter a subject and message – submit the form to see the message appear on the message board

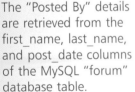

Don't forget

The "Posted By" details are retrieved from the first_name, last_name, and post_date columns of the MySQL "forum" database table.

2 Next, return to the Post Message page then enter only a subject title and submit the form to see an error

Hot tip

You can stop the MySQL Server service and post an empty form to see the MySQL error report.

3 Now, log in as different users and submit more messages to see them get added to the message board

Beware

New forum messages are added to the bottom of the table here but the order could be reversed by adding a SORT clause to the SQL query.

Summary

- User messages can be stored in a MySQL database table and retrieved later for display on a forum page

- Typically, a MySQL database forum table might store the post id, user's names, subject, message, and date of posting

- Forum pages are often only available to registered users so the PHP script providing a forum page will check for user login

- A forum page will display a list of posted messages or advise that there are currently no messages

- The forum page can include a hyperlink to a page where the user can post new messages to the forum

- A form to post forum messages will submit the subject and message to a PHP script for processing

- The script processing posted messages stores the submitted subject and message data in a MySQL database table when the data is valid and the post attempt succeeds

- The script processing posted messages also stores user details from session data in the MySQL database table together with the date and time that the message was posted by the user

- PHP scripts to process messages posted to a forum should supply an error message when the post attempt fails

- The script producing a forum page can retrieve the user's names, date of posting, subject, and message body for each message stored in a MySQL database table

- Forum messages can be displayed in individual rows of a table on the forum page

10 Processing shops

This chapter builds on the previous two chapters to demonstrate how to create a simple e-commerce shopping cart application.

Creating a shop database

Item details can be stored in a MySQL database table for display in a shop page containing items for selection by registered users. Typically, a database table containing shop items might store the item's ID, name, description, an illustrative image path and price:

Column Name:	Content Type:	Example:
item_id	Number	1
item_name	Text	Cow
item_desc	Text	A meadow mate
item_img	Text	images/cow.png
item_price	Decimal	10.00

The design of this database table requires that **VARCHAR** data types should be specified for columns storing text. Item IDs should be positive (**UNSIGNED**) integer **INT** values that the table automatically allocates with **AUTO_INCREMENT,** and the price should be stored as a **DECIMAL(4,2)** value. All details will be required to store an item in the database table so each column must have a **NOT NULL** rule.

The SQL command required to produce this design as a MySQL database table named "shop" can be issued at the prompt in the MySQL Command Line Client, or saved in an SQL file which can be implemented by issuing the **SOURCE** command.

The table can then be populated with items by issuing a further command describing each required item detail.

create_shop.sql

1. Launch a plain text editor and create an SQL command describing the table requirements shown above
```
CREATE TABLE IF NOT EXISTS shop (
item_id INT UNSIGNED NOT NULL AUTO_INCREMENT ,
item_name VARCHAR(20) NOT NULL ,
item_desc VARCHAR(200) NOT NULL ,
item_img VARCHAR(20) NOT NULL ,
item_price DECIMAL(4,2) NOT NULL ,
PRIMARY KEY ( item_id ) ) ;
```

2 Now, create an SQL command to populate the table

```
INSERT INTO shop
( item_name , item_desc , item_img , item_price )
VALUES
( "Cow" , "A friendly field buddy." ,
                    "images/cow.png" , 19.99 ) ,
( "Dog" , "A friendly lap buddy." ,
                    "images/dog.png" , 14.99 ) ,
( "Goat" , "A friendly mountain buddy." ,
                    "images/goat.png" , 16.99 ) ,
 ( "Leopard" , "A friendly spotted buddy." ,
                    "images/leopard.png" , 17.99 ) ,
( "Rhino" , "A friendly jungle buddy." ,
                    "images/rhino.png" , 29.99 ) ;
```

Hot tip

Notice how the table can be populated with multiple items in a single command by specifying their data groups as a comma-separated list.

3 Save the file as **create_shop.sql** then launch the MySQL Command Line Client as the root user and issue a command to use the established database

```
USE site_db ;
```

4 Now, implement the SQL command by stating the source path to the SQL file on your system, such as

```
SOURCE C:\Users\Mike\Desktop\create_shop.sql
```

5 Finally, issue a command to confirm the table format and to see all the items it contains

```
EXPLAIN shop ; SELECT * FROM shop ;
```

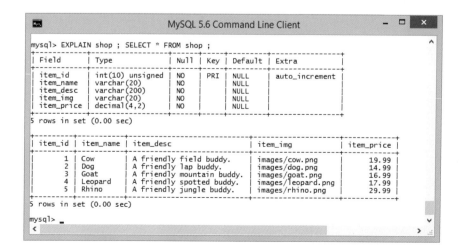

Creating an orders database

Items selected by the user on a shop page for order can best be stored in two MySQL database tables – allowing the user to select multiple items in multiple orders if they so wish.

The first table simply contains summary details of order ID, user ID, total value, and the date on which the order was placed:

Column Name:	Content Type:	Example:
order_id	Number	8
user_id	Number	123
total	Decimal	20.00
order_date	Date/Time	2013-02-14 12:30:00

The second table contains content details of the actual items selected by content ID, order ID, item ID, quantity, and price:

Column Name:	Content Type:	Example:
content_id	Number	100
order_id	Number	8
item_id	Number	1
quantity	Number	2
price	Decimal	10.00

Hot tip

Notice that this shopping cart application utilizes four tables (users, shop, orders, order_contents) perfectly demonstrating the "relational" aspect of MySQL databases.

The **order_id, content_id,** and **order_date** columns are generated by MySQL. The **user_id** is supplied by the "users" table for the current logged-in user, and the **item_id** is supplied by the "shop" table for the selected item. Submission of the shopping cart supplies the **price** and **quantity** from which the **total** is calculated.

1 Launch a plain text editor and create an SQL command describing the first table requirements shown opposite
CREATE TABLE IF NOT EXISTS orders (
order_id INT UNSIGNED NOT NULL AUTO_INCREMENT ,
user_id INT UNSIGNED NOT NULL ,
total DECIMAL(8,2) NOT NULL ,
order_date DATETIME NOT NULL ,
PRIMARY KEY (order_id)) ;

create_orders.sql

2 Save the file as **create_orders.sql** then create an SQL command describing the second table requirements
CREATE TABLE IF NOT EXISTS order_contents (
content_id INT UNSIGNED NOT NULL AUTO_INCREMENT ,
order_id INT UNSIGNED NOT NULL ,
item_id INT UNSIGNED NOT NULL ,
quantity INT UNSIGNED NOT NULL DEFAULT 1,
price DECIMAL(4,2) NOT NULL ,
PRIMARY KEY (content_id)) ;

create_order_contents.sql

3 Save the second file as **create_order_contents.sql** then launch the MySQL Command Line Client as the root user and issue a command to use the established database
USE site_db ;

4 Now, implement the SQL commands by stating the source path to the SQL files and confirm the table format
SOURCE C:\Users\Mike\Desktop\create_orders.sql
SOURCE C:\Users\Mike\Desktop\create_order_contents.sql
EXPLAIN orders ; EXPLAIN order_contents ;

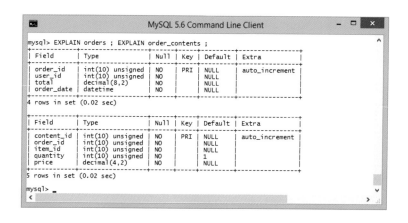

Providing a shop page

Having created the "shop" database, described on pages 170/171, you can now create the PHP script to display all items that may be selected for addition to the shopping cart. Each item will be displayed on the shop page in a table cell containing the item details, and its associated image, together with a hyperlink for adding that item to the shopping cart.

shop.php

1 Launch a plain text editor and begin a PHP script with a statement to allow access to session data

```php
<?php

session_start() ;
```

2 Now, add statements to redirect the browser to the login page if the user is not already logged in

```php
if ( !isset( $_SESSION[ 'user_id' ] ) )
{
  require ( 'login_tools.php' ) ;
  load() ;
}
```

3 Next, add statements to set the page title and include a page header

```php
$page_title = 'Shop' ;
include ( 'includes/header.html' ) ;
```

4 Add a statement to open the database connection

```php
require ( '..\connect_db.php' ) ;
```

Don't forget

The user must be logged in to access this page so their user ID can identify them when placing an order from the shop.

5 Now, add statements to retrieve all items from the database or provide a default message

```php
$q = "SELECT * FROM shop" ;
$r = mysqli_query( $dbc , $q ) ;
if ( mysqli_num_rows( $r ) > 0 )
{
  # Statements to be inserted here (step 6).
}
else
{
  echo '<p>There are currently no items in this shop.</p>' ;
}
```

6 Next, insert statements displaying all items retrieved from the database table then closing the database connection

```
echo '<table><tr>' ;
while ( $row = mysqli_fetch_array( $r , MYSQLI_ASSOC ) )
{
  echo '<td><strong>' . $row['item_name'] .
  '</strong><br>' . $row['item_desc'] .
  '<br><img src=' . $row['item_img'] .
  '><br>$' . $row['item_price'] .
  '<br><a href="added.php?id=' . $row['item_id'] .
  '">Add To Cart</a></td>';
}
echo '</tr></table>' ;
mysqli_close( $dbc ) ;
```

Hot tip

Notice that the hyperlink to add an item to the cart appends the item ID when the link is followed – so the target page can identify the item.

7 Add a statement to create hyperlinks to other pages on the website, including a "View Cart" page

```
echo '<p><a href="cart.php">View Cart</a> |
<a href="forum.php">Forum</a> |
<a href="home.php">Home</a> |
<a href="goodbye.php">Logout</a></p>' ;
```

8 Add a final statement to include a page footer

```
include ( 'includes/footer.html' ) ;
```

9 Save this script in your web browser's **/htdocs** directory as **shop.php** then log in and visit the shop page

175

Don't forget

The illustrative image files, such as "cow.png" must be contained in a folder named "images" located in your web server's **/htdocs** directory.

Confirming cart additions

Having provided the shop page, described on the previous pages, you now create the PHP script that will store items selected by the user in a session variable array. This will use the item's ID number, appended in the "Add To Cart" hyperlink, to retrieve the associated item name from the "shop" database table for display in a confirmation message that the item has been added to the cart.

added.php

1 Launch a plain text editor and begin a PHP script with a statement to allow access to session data
```php
<?php

session_start() ;
```

2 Now, add statements to redirect the browser to the login page if the user is not already logged in
```php
if ( !isset( $_SESSION[ 'user_id' ] ) )
{
  require ( 'login_tools.php' ) ;
  load() ;
}
```

3 Next, add statements to set the page title and include a page header
```php
$page_title = 'Cart Addition' ;
include ( 'includes/header.html' ) ;
```

Don't forget

The ID number of the selected item is appended to the URL of this web page by the shop page's PHP script.

4 Assign the passed item ID to a variable
```php
if ( isset( $_GET['id'] ) ) $id = $_GET['id'] ;
```

5 Now, add a statement to open the database connection
```php
require ( '..\connect_db.php' ) ;
```

6 Next, add statements to retrieve the selected item's data from the database
```php
$q = "SELECT * FROM shop WHERE item_id = $id " ;
$r = mysqli_query( $dbc , $q ) ;
if ( mysqli_num_rows( $r ) == 1 )
{
  $row = mysqli_fetch_array( $r , MYSQLI_ASSOC ) ;

  # Statements to be inserted here (step 7).
}
```

7 Insert statements to add the selected item to the cart and display an appropriate confirmation message

```php
if ( isset( $_SESSION['cart'][$id] ) )
{
  $_SESSION['cart'][$id]['quantity']++ ;
  echo '<p>Another '.$row["item_name"].
        ' has been added to your cart</p>';
}
else
{
  $_SESSION['cart'][$id]=
    array ( 'quantity' => 1, 'price' => $row['item_price'] ) ;
  echo '<p>A '.$row["item_name"].
        ' has been added to your cart</p>' ;
}
```

Hot tip

Notice that the cart array quantity is set to 1 and its price is set when the first item with that ID gets added, otherwise its quantity is simply incremented by 1.

8 Next, add a statement to close the database connection

```php
mysqli_close( $dbc ) ;
```

9 Now, add a statement to create hyperlinks to other pages on the website

```php
echo '<p><a href="shop.php">Shop</a> |
<a href="cart.php">View Cart</a> |
<a href="forum.php">Forum</a> |
<a href="home.php">Home</a> |
<a href="goodbye.php">Logout</a></p>' ;
```

10 Add a final statement to include a page footer

```php
include ( 'includes/footer.html' ) ;
```

11 Save this script in your web browser's **/htdocs** directory as **added.php** then add an item to the cart on the shop page

Beware

Reloading this web page in your browser will once more pass the selection to the script – increasing its cart quantity again.

177

Processing shopping carts

Having provided a page to confirm addition of a selected item to the shopping cart, described on the previous pages, you can now create the PHP script that will display a summary of all selections. This will use the session data to create a table of selected items and quantities, retrieve their associated name and description from the database, calculate a total, and allow quantities to be updated.

cart.php

1 Launch a plain text editor and begin a PHP script with a statement to allow access to session data

```php
<?php

session_start() ;
```

2 Now, add statements to redirect the browser to the login page if the user is not already logged in

```php
if ( !isset( $_SESSION[ 'user_id' ] ) )
{
  require ( 'login_tools.php' ) ;
  load() ;
}
```

3 Next, add statements to set the page title and include a page header

```php
$page_title = 'Cart' ;
include ( 'includes/header.html' ) ;
```

Don't forget

The user might enter a non-numeric value into the quantity update field so the script must ensure the quantity field value is indeed an integer.

4 Add statements to update the quantities if the page has been submitted for amendment

```php
if ( $_SERVER['REQUEST_METHOD'] == 'POST' )
{
  foreach ( $_POST['qty'] as $item_id => $item_qty )
  {
    # Ensure values are integers.
    $id = (int) $item_id ;
    $qty = (int) $item_qty ;

    # Change quantity or delete if zero.
    if ( $qty == 0 )
    { unset ( $_SESSION['cart'][$id] ) ; }
    elseif ( $qty > 0 )
    { $_SESSION['cart'][$id]['quantity'] = $qty ; }
  }
}
```

5 Now, initialize a grand total variable
```
$total = 0 ;
```

6 Next, add a statement to display the contents of the shopping cart, or display a message if the cart is empty
```
if ( !empty( $_SESSION['cart'] ) )
{
   # Statements to be inserted here (steps 7-11).
}
else
{ echo '<p>Your cart is currently empty.</p>' ; }
```

Hot tip

The **foreach** loop adds each item ID plus a comma to the query, and the **substr()** function removes the final comma.

7 Insert a first statement to open the database connection
```
require ( '../connect_db.php' ) ;
```

8 Next, insert statements to retrieve data from the "shop" database for all associated items in the shopping cart
```
$q = "SELECT * FROM shop WHERE item_id IN (" ;
foreach ( $_SESSION['cart'] as $id => $value )
{ $q .= $id . ',' ; }
$q = substr( $q , 0 , -1 ) . ') ORDER BY item_id ASC' ;
$r = mysqli_query ( $dbc , $q ) ;
```

9 Now, insert statements to display the cart selections in a form that contains a table
```
echo '<form action="cart.php" method="POST"><table>
<tr><th colspan="5">Items in your cart</th></tr><tr>' ;

while ( $row = mysqli_fetch_array ( $r , MYSQLI_ASSOC ) )
{
   # Calculate sub-totals and grand total.
   $subtotal = $_SESSION['cart'][$row['item_id']]['quantity']
        * $_SESSION['cart'][$row['item_id']]['price'] ;
   $total += $subtotal ;

   # Display the row.
   echo "<tr> <td>{$row['item_name']}</td>
   <td>{$row['item_desc']}</td>
   <td><input type=\"text\" size=\"3\"
   name=\"qty[{$row['item_id']}]\"
   value=\"{$_SESSION['cart'][$row['item_id']]['quantity']}\">
   </td> <td>@ {$row['item_price']} = </td>
   <td>".number_format ( $subtotal , 2 )."</td></tr>" ;
}
```

Hot tip

The SQL **ORDER BY** clause will ensure the selected items are displayed in the order of their number ID.

...cont'd

10 Insert a statement to display the grand total at the end of the table and a submit button at the end of the form

```
echo ' <tr><td colspan="5">
Total = '.number_format( $total , 2 ).'</td></tr>
</table>
<input type="submit" value="Update My Cart">
</form>' ;
```

Don't forget

Appending the total value to the checkout page URL enables that page to confirm that the cart is not empty.

11 Now, insert a statement to close the database connection

```
mysqli_close( $dbc ) ;
```

12 Add a statement to create hyperlinks to other pages on the website, including a "Checkout" page that appends the grand total to the URL

```
echo '<p><a href="shop.php">Shop</a> |
 <a href="checkout.php?total='.$total.'">Checkout</a> |
<a href="forum.php">Forum</a> |
<a href="home.php">Home</a> |
<a href="goodbye.php">Logout</a></p>' ;
```

13 Add a final statement to include a page footer

```
include ( 'includes/footer.html' ) ;
```

14 Save this script in your web browser's **/htdocs** directory as **cart.php** then select items on the shop page and view the cart to see the selection details and values

15 Now, change the value in the quantity field of one of the items and click the Update button to see the revised cart

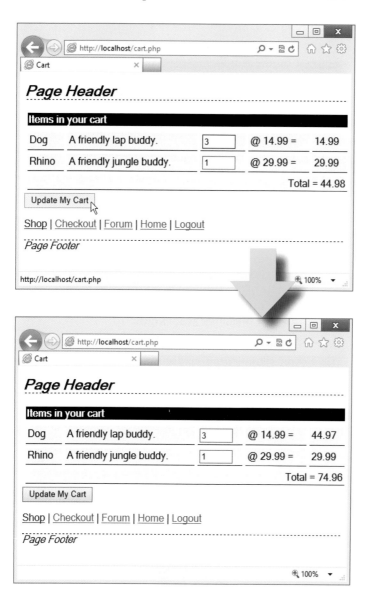

Hot tip

You can change all quantities to zero and click the Update button to see the default empty cart message.

Checking out orders

Having produced a shopping cart page, described on the previous pages, you can now create a PHP script to process the user's selected items as a "checkout" order. This is the culmination of the shopping cart process and will store the cart selections in the "order" and "order_contents" database tables for subsequent fulfillment by the supplier.

checkout.php

1 Launch a plain text editor and begin a PHP script with a statement to allow access to session data
```
<?php
  session_start() ;
```

2 Now, add statements to redirect the browser to the login page if the user is not already logged in
```
if ( !isset( $_SESSION[ 'user_id' ] ) )
{ require ( 'login_tools.php' ) ;  load() ; }
```

3 Next, add statements to set the page title and include a page header
```
$page_title = 'Checkout' ;
include ( 'includes/header.html' ) ;
```

Don't forget

The total value of the shopping cart is appended to the URL of this web page by the cart page's PHP script.

4 Add statements to store the shopping cart items in the database or provide a default message
```
if ( isset( $_GET['total'] )
        && ( $_GET['total'] > 0 )
        && ( !empty( $_SESSION['cart'] ) ) )
{
    # Statements to be inserted here (steps 5-10).
}
else
{ echo '<p>There are no items in your cart.</p>' ; }
```

5 Now, insert a statement to open the database connection
```
require ( '../connect_db.php' ) ;
```

6 Next, insert statements to store the user ID, total order value, and current date/time in the "orders" database table
```
$q =
"INSERT INTO orders ( user_id , total , order_date ) VALUES ("
. $_SESSION['user_id']."," .$_GET['total'].", NOW() ) " ;
$r = mysqli_query ( $dbc , $q ) ;
```

7 Insert a statement to retrieve the current order number

```
$order_id = mysqli_insert_id( $dbc ) ;
```

8 Now, add statements to retrieve the selected cart item details from the "shop" database

```
$q = "SELECT * FROM shop WHERE item_id IN (" ;
foreach ( $_SESSION['cart'] as $id => $value )
{ $q .= $id . ',' ; }
$q = substr( $q , 0 , -1 ) . ') ORDER BY item_id ASC' ;
$r = mysqli_query ( $dbc , $q ) ;
```

Hot tip

The **foreach** loop adds each item ID plus a comma to the query, and the **substr()** function removes the final comma.

9 Next, insert statements to store the item details in the "order_contents" database

```
while ( $row = mysqli_fetch_array ( $r , MYSQLI_ASSOC ) )
{
  $query = "INSERT INTO order_contents
        ( order_id, item_id, quantity, price )
        VALUES ( $order_id , ".$row['item_id'].",".
        $_SESSION['cart'][$row['item_id']]['quantity'].",".
        $_SESSION['cart'][$row['item_id']]['price'].")" ;
  $result = mysqli_query( $dbc , $query ) ;
}
```

10 Insert statements to close the database connection, display a confirmation message, and empty the cart

```
mysqli_close( $dbc ) ;
echo "<p>Thanks for your order.
        Your Order Number Is #".$order_id."</p>" ;
$_SESSION['cart'] = NULL ;
```

11 Add a statement to create hyperlinks to other pages on the website, including a "Logout" page

```
echo '<p><a href="shop.php">Shop</a> |
<a href="forum.php">Forum</a> |
<a href="home.php">Home</a> |
<a href="goodbye.php">Logout</a></p>' ;
```

Beware

Payment processing is not included in this example but could be added before the checkout has ended.

12 Add a final statement to include a page footer

```
include ( 'includes/footer.html' ) ;
```

13 Save this script in your web browser's **/htdocs** directory as **checkout.php** to complete the shopping cart application

Confirming logout success

Having produced a checkout page, described on the previous pages, you can now create a PHP script to allow the user to log out from the website. This destroys all session data so the user cannot access the website without logging in once more.

goodbye.php

1 Launch a plain text editor and begin a PHP script with a statement to allow access to session data
```
<?php

session_start() ;
```

2 Now, add statements to redirect the browser to the login page if the user is not already logged in
```
if ( !isset( $_SESSION[ 'user_id' ] ) )
{ require ( 'login_tools.php' ) ;  load() ; }
```

3 Next, add statements to set the page title and include a page header
```
$page_title = 'Goodbye' ;
include ( 'includes/header.html' ) ;
```

4 Add a statement to clear existing session variables
```
$_SESSION = array() ;
```

5 Now, add a statement to end the session
```
session_destroy() ;
```

6 Next, add a statement to display a confirmation message and provide a hyperlink back to the login page
```
echo '<h1>Goodbye!</h1>
<p>You are now logged out.</p>
<p><a href="login.php">Login</a></p>' ;
```

7 Finally, add a statement to include a page footer
```
include ( 'includes/footer.html' ) ;
```

8 Save the script in your web browser's **/htdocs** directory as **goodbye.php** then select items from the shop, checkout, then log out from the website

Don't forget

By default, a session does not end until the user closes their browser – so the PHP script must end the session when the user logs out.

184

Hot tip

You could easily extend the checkout page script to include order details.

PHP and MySQL are a flexible, powerful combination that have an important role to fill in the future of the Web.

Summary

- Item details can be stored in a MySQL database table for display in a shop page containing items for selection

- Typically, a database table containing shop items might store the item ID, name, description, image path, and price

- Order details can be stored in two related MySQL database tables allowing selection of multiple items in multiple orders

- Typically, a database table containing order summary details might store the order ID, user ID, total value, and order date

- A database table containing order content details might store the content ID, order ID, user ID, quantity, and price

- A shop item can be added to the shopping cart by appending its ID to a hyperlink to the cart page

- Details of items in a shopping cart can be stored in a session variable array

- Session data can be used to create a table of selected items and quantities by retrieving their associated name and description

- A PHP script to display shopping cart contents can calculate the total value and be easily updated by the user

- Checkout stores the items in a shopping cart as an order in related database tables containing order summary and contents

- A supplier can retrieve order details stored in a MySQL database to subsequently fulfill orders

- A PHP logout script must destroy all session data so the user cannot access the website until they log in once more

Index

191

T

U

V

W

X

Z